How money works.word v10odt

Tiger Moth

How money works- *and why you can't get enough of it*

This is the most important topic ...we all need money...it is the heart of the Capitalist system...without money...which is the oil in a car...or the blood in the circulatory system... keeps the economy moving and keeps you alive.

Money has been around over thousand years in many forms...coins...beads...shells…cigarettes (during the Second world War).It has been used to trade in all sorts of goods and services...as a store of value...each unit of currency must be the same ..i.e. uniform.

Today money comes in three forms (1) currency created by Central banks...the cash we use (2) by private banks…created as debt...also other various financial institutions (3) Central banks also create money as debt...there is also the credit system...and businesses like Facebook creating its own money…and digital coins like bitcoin...and the original money…gold and silver little used today.

This most important subject needs a thorough understanding...without which you will always be at the mercy of Financial con men and the government who want to tax you to death...for your own good...let the story begin

The Ascent of Money and the decline of economics

Before money we used to barter…we exchanged things… for things we wanted...so i might want a cow for say 10 chickens...or wheat...or i swapped my wife for your wife...and so on...barter however has limits...what if i didn't like your wife.

As time went on we got more sophisticated (some of us)…we exchanged more things…however once coins were invented we could buy a lot more things and keep a proper record of our transactions...more wives and other things became available...as long as you had the money.

The first economist was ..a parrot called 'failure'…learned to say supply and demand...the economics profession has yet to recover from the reputation of this parrot...economics now best described as the failed profession...intention to make us all rich...not done a good job.

Supply and demand is the bedrocks of the capitalist system...production creates demand...too much and prices drop...too little prices go up...the right amount of production and consumption is more art than science

The best is to get to the median level where prices fluctuate within a narrow band...i.e. affordable for the average consumer and for business to supply and produce.

Today the amount of money in existence is in excess of $80.9 trillion dollars...yet we have much poverty in the mist of so much money...poverty should be history

- macroeconomics...is concerned with the total money in the economy...i.e. GDP which includes your wages...unemployment and other economic activity in the country
- microeconomics...is about firms and people...economic activity in your local area
- today as money is becoming digital...our relationship to money will also changing
- if money is numbers on a computer screen...why cannot we give everybody enough to live on?
- Barter being the first form of trading had limits...both parties must have something to exchange...setting the value can be difficult...limited to local areas due to transportation and other factors
- the benefits were...you exchanged actual goods...created long lasting trading relationships with others
- barter still exists today... in an informal way...when you mow your elderly neighbours garden and he looks after your property...when you are on holiday...no cash is exchanged...only a tacit understanding...that is barter
- (source:dk publishing how money works)

IOU'S

- For farmers these were ideal settlement of trade...so some growing wheat once harvested could exchange for a cow reared by another farmer...as no cash was needed upfront or exchanged
- these iou's were in written form... or understanding and could be exchanged for goods...first legal documents
- as the iou's had a value they could be exchanged for other things than for the original purchase
- in fact, they acted like money...we have the same today called the credit system today

The many forms of money

Money to be valid for trade and commerce must have a certain number properties:-

- it must be durable...paper is less durable than coinage
- it must be portable...too large it can be difficult to transport
- it must uniform and divisible...each $dollar must be the same
- it must be used for exchange...that is it must be acceptable in your country and maybe in other countries
- it must be limited in supply...something Central banks have yet to learn this...with all the money printing
- barter started first...the Sumerian's were first to record transactions on tablets...which acted as receipts...this may happen again if we have nuclear war
- cowrie shells were used as means of exchange in India and the South Pacific...might be a good idea to have a supply of cowrie shells...the future is uncertain
- the smart Greeks minted Silver coins used across the Greek Empire...silver is still a good investment...if you have any ...hold on to it.
- (source:dk publishing how money works)

What is money for

The Sociologist Simmel was the first to publish our relationship to money...in the past people made goods...but difficult to assign value...money solved this problem...able to assign value...more transactions could take place...hence more freedom and choice in the market place. Money has to perform the following functions:-

- **store of value**...must not be perishable...which the Colombian drug cartel was to find out when...millions of $dollars wrapped in plastic had deteriorated in the humid jungle where it had been stored

- **as a means of exchange**...it must be acceptable for purchases at all locations...it can be divided...so change can be given...it must be stable in value...otherwise it will cause chaos with your budget

- **it must be a unit of account**...so we can work out who is the richest person in the world...most likely not you or me...only a single authority like the State should be allowed to issue it ..hence gives the money trust and value...however with bitcoin and other exchange money in circulation...we are in new and uncertain monetary world

- The Chinese Han dynasty used copper coins with hole punched in the middle...useful...used less copper...more coins...can be strung...carrying made easy... and made lots of noise while walking

- The Byzantine Empire made coins of pure gold...bravo the ultimate money...later on they started to dilute the coins with copper...this is known as...the debasement of the money supply...enables you to make more coins with less value...which buys you less due to inflation...something we are all familiar with today

- the Arab Dirham first appeared in silver form 900ce...today it is now paper and digital...silver used as jewellery and investment today...still a good investment

- (source:dk publishing how money works)

How money fuels the economy

The evolution of money is an interesting one. In the 17th century banks were created to regulate the money supply (they are not doing a good job today)...in the 20th century the link between the paper money and gold..i.e. the gold standard was delinked...first by the UK then the US in the 1970's ...today there is no link between precious metals and paper money...and many of our economic problems

There is now a wide variety of money forms

From coins...to precious metals ...to paper money...credit and debit cards...cryptocurrencies...to financial instruments such as derivatives... a short history of money as follows:-

- the Spanish discovered and destroyed the new World...now called Latin America...they found Gold and Silver...used slave labour to dig the stuff...sent 350 tons between 1540-1640 back to Europe
- this made the Crown and a few parasites rich ...fuelled inflation as increase in money not related rise in goods and services...this is the first known effect of excessive money supply in Europe...made life difficult for the mass of Spanish people...i.e. the cost-of-living crises...which we are all familiar with today
- in little old England fat slob King Henry V111 ...besides having a bad attitude towards women...debased the silver coinage by mixing with copper ...yes... you've guessed it...caused inflation...lots of unhappy subjects...trust in the money supply drops along with the Crown
- in the 1970's the US increased the price of wheat...at that time the US was the world's largest wheat supplier...the Gulf oil producers in retaliation increased the price of oil...this caused massive inflation...Western industry was so reliant on oil...for industry and transport...it took decades to recover
- when little old England was an Empire in 1844...it set the gold standard...where a certain amount of £pounds equal

to so much gold…this lasted for over 200 years…until world war one and two finished the British Empire…replaced by the new US Empire…which is now coming to an end

- in the 1970's credit cards were invented enabling people to buy now and pay a lot later with high interest rates…also allow people to spread their purchases in instalments…over a longer period
- the credit innovation has led to a rise of personal debt…where some people now use it recklessly to fund a lifestyle they cannot afford…personal debt they cannot pay back...personal bankruptcies at an all-time high
- in the 1990's electronic transfer of money…means money has become digital…for business it is a great convenience…lowers transaction costs…safer than handling large amounts of cash
- with mobile communication and the internet…the convenience of digital banking and payments is available to all those who have access to this technology…a great technological leap forward
- (source:dk publishing how money works)

Gresham's Law

Thomas Gresham's law…***good money drives out bad money***…he observed when governments debased the money supply…i.e. coins with less gold and silver content…people will keep the good coins with high precious metal content and spend the bad money…this is a good principle to live by in other aspects of your life…keep the good stuff …and get rid of the crap in your house on eBay.

- in 1553 in little old England the first joint stock company created…or the modern corporation where shares sold in companies…who conduct trade…lie…cheat and steal other countries resources…the most evil company during the colonial period being the East India company…which had its own army.

- The royal mint responsible for minting coins in 1696...they have been minting worthless...useless...depreciating coins and notes since then...someone must stop them doing this
- 1999 the EU empire created its own currency the Euro to replace members currency...the Greeks come to regret this...when their economy crashes

Modern economics...trade and investment

Trade expanded during the period of colonialism...Imperialism and economic development of the European continent at the expense of everyone else. Adam Smith... he of the 'invisible' hand fame...proposed the role of the government to be limited...to facilitate freedom of trade...people pursuing their own self-interest will make everyone happier and richer...and we all get what we want in life...today this means increasing debt and taxes

Applying this today we can definitely say Bill Gates and Jeff Bezos are richer and happier than the rest of us...we however do what we can with higher living costs...lower wages...more personal debt.

The 'invisible hand' has been replaced by the visible hand of big governments to tax us at gun point...and corporations who want to make as much profit as possible out of us...the best way to form cartels...rig markets...monopolies...oligopolies...investor rights agreements dressed up as free trade agreements sold to the public as for their benefit

- Adam Smith's simple trade model is...if seller A charges too much.. it will encourage new entrants unless it has monopoly position...i.e. can rig the market
- new entrant seller B will sell at a lower price than seller A...he gets all the customers and profit
- in reality this does not happen often...limits to entry... may be tariffs on imported goods...and other factors...it is very difficult to dis-lodge an existing trader from a market dominant position

- in the real world a country will give considerable protection to its key industry...as countries are doing today...the EU and the US among the worst offenders
- in the past little old England passed the navigation act...which outlawed any trade between it and its colonies in ships in non-UK ships...this is known as mercantilism...which the US accuses China of today
- **Market Equilibrium**...this means when quantities of goods by sellers and buyers satisfies consumer demand in a fair price for all...in the real world...business charge what they can get away with...people's incomes are limited...they stop buying when their money runs out...which is quicker than the quantity of goods and services in the market place
- **Laissez-faire**...French word for let it be...caused nothing but problems for the world...principle that no government interference in the market place will lead to best outcomes for people in providing goods and services...at an optimal level...not done so well lately with all the market crashes...Laissez Faire should be replaced with let's be stupid and let markets destroy us all in taxpayer bail outs
- **Comparative advantage**...countries should specialize in what they are good at...applying this principle... China should be exporting rice...not electric cars...France should be exporting wine...not industrial goods...etc...another nutty idea past its sell by date...a country can produce whatever it wants...if it has the resources...manpower...technology...and markets to sell to ...South Korea has proven this in shipbuilding in which it had no comparative to do so.

(source:dk publishing how money works)

Measuring the economy-only for fool's or economists

Interest in how the flow and quantity money in circulation effects prices...consumers and business has been a rich fertile ground of study:-

- John Maynard Keynes argued that government spending and taxation affects prices...more than the money supply
- he proposed during a recession...government must spend money on public works...this will stimulate demand...lower unemployment...the multiplier effect create more money and demand than the initial inputs
- in the real-world Politicians make promises to voters which they cannot afford...they borrow money not for productive investment... but paying higher pensions and welfare payments
- these loans incur interest payments which future generations and those not yet born will pay for
- the original loans are never paid off...only the interest...at some future date the lenders may decide not to lend...or lend less money...leading to crises...as happened to Greece...when total debt exceeds the GDP of a country...it is in effect bankrupt...even if it continues to pay interest on the debt
- Keynes argued for government spending in bad times to stimulate the economy...and the money paid back in the good times...that is not what is being done today...reckless Keynesianism
- (source:dk publishing how money works)

Fisher's demand and supply

- **less money in system** equals... we need more money... more stuff to buy
- **more money in system** equals... we need less money equals less demand equals...we buy less
- in the real world most of us never have enough money for all the goods we need...after paying for essentials...what's left is for discretionary spending...which can rise and fall.

Marx theory of value

- the value of goods determined by how much labour is used ...not the demand for it

- a table takes 5 hours to make at $10 per hour-table costs - $50
- in the real world you well know that you have no value...the employer wants the cheapest labour possible...that is you or someone else...this is known as 'race to the bottom'

  In the 16th century people noticed that an abundance of silver from the New World(or slave colonies of Europe)...prices of goods and services increased

  - Two views emerged in the 20th century how to deal with this situation...(1)one group let the market decide...the equilibrium theory (2)second group...government intervention to maintain a healthy economic balance...the government by tax and spend can create demand in the economy

Hayek's business cycle

- in a recession... interest rates fall...this leads to expansion of the money supply...to counter the excessive demand in the economy interest rates must rise

Tiger Moto's poverty cycle

- when money is cheap...low interest rates...people borrow to spend on consumer goods rather than in productive investment...like starting a business
- endless property speculation and consumer spending...sends prices beyond their underlying values
- this leads to rampant inflation
- governments then increase interest rates...first by small amounts ...which has little effect...then large rises
- this leads to reduced demand and rising unemployment
- you now have to pay back loans with higher interest payments
- since your wages do not rise to compensate for the rise in interest rates

- you are now made poorer...in some cases absolutely poor if you lose your job or business

Friedman money cycle

- if interest rates low…people can borrow more...spend more in the shops...economy expands...everyone is a winner
- if interest rates too high...people will save some of their money and spend the rest in the shops…since shops have less money...they pay less to suppliers and workers...everyone is a loser...accept the banks
- in the real world by having a citizen's income...we can have high or low interest rates… which will not affect the ordinary people much...as there will be a minimum purchasing power in the economy

The Business cycle

- as the economy expands business increase production to meet demand
- business invests in increased production...opening new factories and shops…hire more people
- with increased production and consumption and rising employment and wages...there is no need for government intervention

    In the real world as the economy expands because of easy credit...production increases but not in your country...because manufacturing is now abroad in China and elsewhere...people's wages do not rise as much...so you are being made poorer as inflation bites

    The government increases interest rates which make you even poorer....there is a saying the 'economy is doing fine...shame about the people'...welcome to Little Old England and the US

Profit is King

Corporate accounting or fraud...depending on how you see the situation is used in many ways...some business borrows and expand...others hold on to cash...i.e. cash reserves

- **cash flow**...this total money flowing in and out of a business...it is good to have a positive cash flow...i.e. more money coming in than going out
- **smoothing earnings**...shareholders like to see a steady increase in earnings...large companies do their best to do this... even by creative accounting or down right fraud...or good management
- **net income**...this the income left after deducting all expenses including high salaries... share options and bonuses to the board...what's left is known as the taxable income...which is siphoned off...in to...off shore tax havens...so that it cannot be taxed...the rich and large corporations do this all the time
- the tax not paid...is paid by you... and in lower... or less public services available...as in the UK where councils have made rubbish bins smaller and collections less frequent
- in 2015 cash reserves held by US companies $1.7 trillion...ask yourself why is this not taxed
- **gearing ratio**...this the cash and assets of a company and the debt as a% percentage...in your case if you are in debt and have few assets...your gearing ratio is very high...for companies and people it's good to have a low gearing ratio...i.e. less debt
- **expenses**...all costs associated with running a business...in your case household bills plus wife and children
- **assets**...this is premises...plant...equipment...but not employees who are a liability on the balance sheet
- **for you**... your assets are your home...if you can afford to buy one...your car plus wife plus children...wife and children can also be a liability on your balance sheet...if

you are divorced...the maintenance payment enforced by the courts will see to that

- **depreciation...**companies will depreciate an asset such as plant and machinery over the lifetime of that asset...this depreciation allowance is tax deductible
- however, this does not apply to non-business...you do depreciate over time as you age...unfortunately there is no depreciation allowance for ageing...only the coffin waits for you.
- **Net income...**this is very important... it is what is left after deducting expenses...it is what is shared out to owners of capital the shareholders...also determines whether company is performing compared to the industry norm...this often referred to as the p/e ratio...which is price over earnings...a useful guide for potential investors

    Net income however can be adjusted to give a better overall picture...creative accounting...that is fraud to you and me. A well-known supermarket in the UK...was inflating earnings by adding future earnings into its accounting data. Enron however went much further...its accounts were total fraud.

    An apple a day keeps the Doctor away and the tax man

    Apple the phone company first quarter profits in 2016 were $18.4 billion...and very little went into tax...all legal...this tells us they have the best accountants and Lawyers in the world.

    In future Apple should not only sell iPhone's but also give tax advice to its customers.

business terminology

- bottom line..net income...what's left after expenses...in your case what's left in your bank account at the end of the month
- **earnings per share**..net income divided by number of shares...or p/e ratio...tells you whether the company is performing well...in your case your wife-partner will let

you know your p/e ratio...the more money you have the better your p/e ratio

- **depreciation of assets**...decline in value of such things as plant and machinery and property...in your case you depreciate as you age...best to slow down the process if you can
- **bank charges and interest payments**...if you borrow ..you pay...in your case... your house loan and personal debt will ensure you will remain a debt slave and wage slave until debts are cleared...your bank will keep you informed regularly of your liabilities to them

Capitalizing expenses

There are two types of expenses (1) revenue...such as electricity and stationery (2) capital expenditure like buying a photo copier...a business needs to decide which it is... and account for it...the inland revenue will decide in many cases allowable expenses

- depending on the asset a company can decide how to account for it... in its accounts...how many years...so a bus company will record an asset to be paid over say ten years...this can affect the profit to be made...if the asset to be recorded in one two years...profit will be reduced considerably
- however, this is open to abuse...some companies by 'creative accounting' have recorded an expense as an investment...and incorporated future earnings in to the accounts not yet earned...this makes the profits earned higher than actual
- for you creative accounting...also known as fraud...is not available as an option...doing so will get you locked up or heavily fined...avoid both if possible
- So, companies can 'adjust' their profits by using a number of accounting 'tricks'...record a purchase in the same year as an expense...reduces profit...and tax liability...or...record the purchase as an asset...and depreciate the asset over a longer period which will smooth

out earnings ...each firm needs to work out what is in its interest.

- (source:dk publishing how money works)

Depreciation...Amortization...and Depletion

As explained earlier that a company has a number of ways to account for an asset purchase...let's looks at the details how this is done:-

- **depreciation**...purchase value less scrap value divided by years of life...applying this in business... a van costing $30,000..scrap value..$5000...useful life 10years=£30,000-$5000/10= $2500 as expense against tax each year

  Applying these formulae to you...life time earning say $2 million $ dollars over 40 years...less tax...50%....at end of your life ..scrap value ..your pension $20,000...once you die ..no pension...scrap value the price of your funeral $5000

- **Amortization**...this often used to write of such things as patents...the cost/divided by the number of years...so a patent costing $20,000 over 10 years =$2000 per year against

  Applying this to you... your patent is your wife-partner...the initial cost... the marriage ..long term costs over 40 years...in buying and running expenses of the house plus any children

- **Depletion**...used in say a forest company which has trees as its resource...as the trees are felled and sold the remaining forest decreases in value and climate damage increase in value

  formulae.... Cost minus salvage value divided by number of years times trees felled equals expense per year

  In your case... cost is the house...paid for over 20 years of your life...a house is a depleting ...deteriorating asset...which will cost more to maintain...salvage value...if you cannot pay the bank loan...it will be repossessed by the bank and sold at a discount...as millions of house owners found out during the 2008 financial crash in the US

In the real-world assets can depreciate or increase in value...a car loses 60% of its value within 3 years...logic do not buy a new car.

Houses on the other hand are one of the few assets that appreciates in value over time as it deteriorates...that is because people speculate on land and property...so called wealth affect...a way of making money without doing anything or knowing anything.

Smoothing earnings...or committing fraud

Shareholders like to see a steady increase in earnings...they do not like to see wild fluctuations...this can disturb not only the shareholders but the market as well...as a sign the company may be in financial trouble.

Companies can in the good years set a side cash reserves for future large purchases and this also helps during the downturn of the economy...this smooths out earnings over a long period...and is good business practice.

However, some companies can also use this accounting practice to hide losses...commit fraud...encourage investors in a company which may not be in a 'healthy' financial position.

- **making a provision** is a good business practice
- a company balance sheet is an income-expenditure statement...assets and liabilities at a given date...it is considered more 'art' than reality
- **profit and loss statement**s...are simply income less expenses...more income happier shareholders...less income...less happy shareholders at the annual general meeting
- **volatility**...as discussed earlier...large increases in income or expenses...positive or negative

    Applying this in the real world to you...making a provision is having savings...if you can...profit and loss is at the end of the month you have more money or less...volatility means you do not have a steady income...this can lead to a very volatile situation with your partner-spouse...you may end up homeless and hungry.

- (source:dk publishing how money works)

Company fraud

Creative accounting can be used to hide all sorts of fraud some of the biggest company frauds are as follows:-

- Enron...$74 billion lost...hidden debts not declared...this is known as off balance sheet recording...or fraud
- WorldCom...inflated its asset values...by almost $11 billion
- Bernie Madoff...offered high rates of returns above market rates...it was a giant Ponzi scheme...investors lost $65 billion...however he was able to keep this con going for a good number of years...yet the authorities never suspected anything
- Lehman Brothers bank...$50 billion in useless...worthless assets...at least the board paid themselves well during this period
- remember the above are known frauds...there are plenty more going on...yet not discovered...one day you might be part of it and not know...like the employees of the above companies

Cash flow...the life blood of business

Without a positive cash flow, no business will survive for long...in simple terms...business makes capital investments at the start of business...and as it trades... cash flow...money coming in...pays expenses...wages...overheads. Loans

- so, in a shop...cash flow pays for stock sold...overheads...like rent...electric...wages...any loan payments...for new equipment and the dreaded tax man...who will make regular visits to your premise to ensure you comply with all tax legislation

Applying this to you...your cash flow is your income...your outgoings...are house hold bills...the house and car loans...the tax authority is your spouse...who will tax you for keeping the house in good order...this tax is non-negotiable...best to pay up and ask no questions...otherwise can lead to a volatile situation

Managing cash flow

Managing cash flow is essential for a business to thrive...however even good companies can get in to financial trouble as follows:-

- **over trading**...a company may do lots of business yet not have enough cash coming in
- **payments not received on time**...this means chasing customers...time consuming and costly
- **invoicing term**s...if you sell on 30 days credit and get paid in 60 days...this will cause cash flow problems...supermarkets are terrible payers 60-90 days is normal...they buy on credit and earn interest on the money...suppliers have been known to go bankrupt
- **declining sales**...shrinking profit margins...this can happen for many reasons...recessions...change in markets...products no longer wanted
- **selling at too low a price**...start up business do this to get market share...very bad strategy...leads to bankruptcy very quickly
- **overheads too high**...expenses of a firm can quickly spiral out of control...if not managed well...very difficult to cut expenses...like staff wages

Applying the above to you...**over trading** means being over worked...ask the junior Doctors in the UK...**payment not received** on time...means your employer finds some excuse to delay payments to you (your wages)...**invoicing terms**...is your employment contract which favours the employer...not you.

declining sales are all the screw ups the management makes...selling at a low price...when prices are dropped to gain market share and does not happen...the staff pay the price...in job losses

high overheads...means the management pay themselves high salaries and bonuses...beyond their actual worth

- Fact... over 80% of all start up business fail...cash flow problems the main reason...so if you want to start a new business make sure you get the money due...hire some 'heavies' to intimidate your customers to pay...the downside you will have no customers...but you will be cash rich.

Business terminology

- **factoring**...where a company sells its invoices...i.e. money due from customers to a factoring firm who pay you a %percentage of the invoice value...anything from 50-70%..this is an act of desperation...as it wipes out any profit you have made
- **accounts payable**...money you owe to other business...the trick is to delay as long as possible
- **accounts receivable**...money due to you from other business...you need this as quickly as possible in your bank account...not theirs
- **ageing schedule**...sorry state of the company... money due and money payable...done every month...a depressing experience as money coming in is less than the money going out
- **cash flow gap** ..as above with why we are not getting paid
- **cash conversion**...a shop will convert stock into cash
- **operating cash flow**...daily movements of money needed to conduct business
- **investing cash flow**...investments...loans...bonds...etc...applies mostly to big business

- **financing cash flow**...money from debtors and creditors...a difficult task to handle if payments not due

In the real-world big business rules...they get maximum benefit in any trade agreement. The supermarkets in the UK...suppliers have a revolving three-month contract...with 60-90 days credit...they determine the prices to be paid ...and any promotions often wholly or partially funded by the suppliers.

Suppliers pay rent for their products on supermarket shelves...if supermarkets order stuff not available from supplier...they are billed for loss of profit...sale or return of products is normal business practice.

As a result of abuse of market power...farmers have gone bankrupt...or no longer supply supermarkets...other suppliers have merged like the meat processing industry...where they have an unwritten agreement to only supply a %percentage of the total needed by the supermarket. This means if they are de-listed they only lose say 10% of their income. Other suppliers who have gone bankrupt or no longer supply supermarkets.

The affect is supermarkets are having to source suppliers from all over the world...this however ever puts them at risk of supply chain disruption...which has happened...so 'shop local...buy local' may be good way to go.

Gearing ratio...nothing to do with cars

In its simplest form is the debt to assets ratio...for a householder it is the loan to asset value of house...the less debt the lower the gearing ratio as percentage...below 25% is considered good.

- **Advantages of debt financing**...it does not affect profitability...tax deductible...can change...the owner retains ownership of company...good for new business short of investors
- **the con**...large debt means if interest rates rise fast...struggle to make repayments...high debt discourage potential investors...loans usually secured on assets...usually the premises...can be sold in event of default.

In the real world there is no free money from banks...banks secure lending before giving any money...in event of default ..they will make you pay...seize your assets...sell them...any shortfall you still owe the bank the money...banks are a necessary evil...we cannot do without.

Most householders who have bank loan...have high gearing ratio...their debt will be very high…the loan to asset value...paid over a lifetime...miss one payment and you can be made bankrupt...with loans now extended to 30 years plus...means you will pay more in interest payments than the value of the house…good news for banks...bad news for the home buyer.

Property loans are safe and secure way for banks to make money...miss a payment your house is up for grab. Companies have to choose (1) borrowing and retain control by the owner (2)issue shares...lose control over the company plus liable for dividends...each company will choose what is in its best interest…some time there is no choice ..if banks will not lend …you have to issue shares to expand.

(source:dk publishing how money works)

Company reports…fact or fiction

Companies produce around two reports per year to let shareholders and potential investors how the company is doing...lots of creative accounting takes place with these reports.

It is not what is in the reports that is the problem ...what is not reported...off balance sheet reporting which hide the true dire state of the company finances

The people who have the up to date and accurate financial facts are the board and management...here's how the scam works:-

- a company will do well in a year...the annual statement by the CEO will say the board and management have done a great job...they deserve their free shares and bonuses

- in a bad year the CEO in his annual report will say...under difficult circumstances the company has done well...the board and management deserve their free shares and bonuses

  The annual report will have a list of headings and figures...here is what they mean:-

- **fixed assets**...intangible like patents...tangible... like premises
- **current asset**s...those that can converted into cash like stock
- **debtors**...people who owe you money
- **creditors**...people you owe money to
- **total assets** less money owing...is net current assets
- number of shares issued
- **retained profits** for the bonuses and share options
- **shareholder fund**…money in the firm for more bonuses and shares

  In the real world applying the above to you :-

- **fixed assets**...your house
- **intangible assets**...your wife-partner
- **current assets** ...your house less loan owing
- **debtors**...people who owe you money for jobs done for family or friends...which you have no chance of collecting
- **creditors**…people you owe money to...a whole list of them...home loan...car loan…credit card debt...tax...etc
- **liabilities**...all the money you owe above plus more
- **net assets**...the equity in your home
- **issued shares**...your wife and children are the main shareholders
- **retained profit**...that goes to your wife-partner

  Financial instruments versus Musical instruments

A financial instrument is anything that can be traded...shares...loans...assets etc. The instrument is usually a legal document such as a share certificate with obligations like dividend payments.

In this respect there is nothing new. Investors will invest in many financial instruments...i.e. a portfolio of investments with possibly insurance to cover losses.

These insurance instruments called derivatives ...which are used to 'hedge'...protect investments...so derivatives...insurance...bonds...loans and unit trusts and hedge funds are all financial instruments used…by sensible investors…to diversify their portfolio and risk

In the real-world derivatives have been used to off load high risk portfolios to investors as sound investments as low risk...who are unaware of the high risk. The 2008 stock market crash was a consequence of financial instruments turned into musical instruments...as investors 'played like a violin.'

In corrupt…dodgy...financial practices...only to be 'played again like a musical instrument' in tax payer bail out.

Beware of financial instruments...they can quickly be turned into musical instrument….and you've guessed it...the public pays for the performance...in tax payer bail outs.

Shares

Buying of shares is a common practice...a company that is floated on the stock exchange will offer shares to anyone at a price...once bought they may fluctuate depending how the company performs. An investor buying a share is looking for growth and dividend payments

Shares are commonly traded in individual companies or as an investment portfolio like a stocks and shares ISA available in the UK...managed by an investment company.

In the real-world shares are only issued once...unless the company issued additional shares to existing shareholders. Once a share is sold…ownership is transferred to new owner and the dividend stream…however the company does not receive any of this money.

So, share dealing itself has become speculation…a company stock might rise and fall…yet it has no effect on the actual company's day to day operations…it will continue to trade…make profits…expand…hire and fire staff.

So, the bidding up of shares is creating demand in the stock market…the high frequency of share trading is driven by need to earn commission on the share dealing.

In the real-world financial markets (better known as Casino's) $billions are traded in stocks and shares every day and not a single $dollar goes to the companies…unless they issue new shares.

At the moment Elon Musk's car company 'Tesla' is overvalued…
..it is worth more than the largest car producers in the world…Toyota and VW group…which manufacture over 20 million cars world-wide per year. However, 'Tesla' produces under one million and barely makes a profit.

The shares of this company are over hyped…gullible investors who believe that Mr Musk has the ' Midas touch'…when they realize that the Tesla car …is nothing more than an overpriced battery shed on wheels…Toyota has just produced an electric car…with better battery life and technology and cheaper than Tesla.

The Chinese who have invested heavily in electric cars…are going to flood the world market with cheap…reliable electric cars.

The only value in Tesla is the brand itself…as for the car ..overpriced…battery shed on wheels…about to be destroyed by the competition. Investors are going to be played like a musical instrument when they realise the truth.

Bonds as in bonded in labour

There are many types of bonds…there are government bonds…bonds issued by firm…by banks…there is also the more familiar as in 'bonded labour' quite common in Pakistan…a common feature of the landlord system of land tenure.

There are also 'bondage sessions' available by ladies who offer personal services (often advertised in public phone booths). All these bonds involve a monetary transaction.

Government bonds are considered the least risky...assumption being a government cannot go bankrupt...hence good for its debt. Company and bank bonds are riskier in case of default or bankruptcy...the bond holders lose their money. Bonds pay a fixed amount say 10% for a fixed period...at the end of which the bond can redeemed for its original value:-

- **Face value**...the original price of the bond
- **market value**...what it is traded for ..higher or lower dependent on the interest rate and which idiot or party is running the country
- **coupon**...the interest rate paid e.g. 10%...not to be confused with milk coupons...which were given to mothers for their children in the UK in the past...the Fathers prefer Alcohol coupons...teenagers prefer 'recreation drugs coupons'

In the real-world governments issue bonds...because they are short of money...by incurring this debt...future tax payers will have to pay the bond price...debt transfer...which is illegal...immoral and unethical and should be outlawed.

Western governments have been selling increasing number of bonds to cover the mismanagement of the economy...the bond market will explode when investors take the decision that a countries capacity to repay the debt is not there ...when this happens the bond yield ..i.e. the interest rate paid has to be very high...or the bond price will rise or decline ...depending how the money markets assess the situation...that day of reckoning is coming....so get out of the bond market as soon as possible...buy gold or silver

Derivatives...another name for defrauding investors

The idea is simple... a way of protecting one's assets or liabilities from future uncertainty...not unlike insurance...for a small amount of money an investor can protect or limit losses of unforeseen events in the future...the various types as follows:-

- **futures contracts**...the trade involves the buyer to pay an agreed price for a commodity in the future...say like oil or wheat...or air lines... that fix the price of fuel
- **options**...this is same as futures contract accept you do not need to buy the commodity...you can sell the option before delivery of commodity...also the initial transaction does not need full amount paid in full

In the real world these two forms of protection for investors traders have turned out not to be very protective. The financial crises of 2008 exposed the flaws.

These derivatives were based on debt leverage...i.e. a small amount of money covering large amount of potential liabilities...also based on complex mathematical models...where risk was not shared but transferred to investors who had no idea of the risks involved.

Baring's Bank went under because a junior trader was allowed to make huge 'bets'... if they went wrong would expose the bank to huge losses...which it did...as a result Barings lost $827million..but the money has gone into other people's pockets...not disappear in the mist...so there are some very happy people who have profited from the demise of Barings...and beware of junior traders.

The derivatives market is another gambling syndicate designed to fleece customers...financial products designed in such a way to confuse customers of the risk...while at the same time convince them of the benefits.

In the UK we had such a situation where banks sold worthless payment protection plans...i.e. defrauded customers...when they were found out...the banks had to pay back the defrauded customers the $billions of dollars

The mainstream media described this as 'mis-selling' by the banks...to you and me they committed fraud...but the British do have unique way of describing fraud.

At this very moment someone in the financial market is designing a new 'financial product' to defraud customers...be warned you could be the next victim.

(source:dk publishing how money works)

Financial markets...or a den of thieves

Financial markets exist to serve the needs of the business community...enabling investors and corporations to raise funds...buy or sell assets...such as shares...bonds...and conduct a variety of other financial transactions like floating a company to go 'public'. All these functions do occur...but with financialization of the world economy...financial centres have been turned into Casino's...The world's leading Casinos are:-

- **New York**...the world's leading money laundering centre
- **London**.. a close second...linked to New York...to launder looted money from developing countries
- **Tokyo**...less laundering...more bankrupting Japan in the world's most expensive land and property speculation...the property bubble burst decades ago ..Japan has yet to recover
- **Toronto**...launder looted money on a smaller scale...laundered and looted money has gone into the local property market...you've guessed it...sky high properties prices...locals priced out of the market...a small number of wealthy East Asians blamed.
- **Shanghai**...Shenzhen and Hong Kong...the first two act as they should...provide finance for industry...Hong Kong gate way to China...laundering money linked to Singapore...it estimated 'flight capital'...polite name for laundered and looted money is in excess of $1 trillion from China...these figures are not verified.
- **The European Union**...designed to fleece EU citizens...does an excellent job...ask the Greeks
- **Frankfurt**...Germany...its financial market to supply finance to its industry...with the Ukraine conflict...no cheap gas or oil from Russia...German industry is

suffering...less will be needed to finance German industry...they can however switch to fleecing their bank customers...and the German citizens.

- Deutche Bank went bankrupt...had to be bailed out by the German tax payer...i hope they get cheap loans from the bank in the future...if not demand the money back or dividends.

In the real world the primary function of Finance to provide for industry...try getting finance to open a factory with payback period of twenty years...not so easy.

If you are a small business and need money for expansion...they will give you less than 70% secured against an asset...and they expect the money repaid between 3- 5years..impossible task...anyone who has been in business will tell you it takes 3-5 years to break even...what the bank is telling you we don't want your business

How ever they involve themselves in financial transactions...like take over a company...providing credit for purchase...they charge a hefty commission...and may get more money when the purchased company is re-organized for sale to another buyer.

Re-organized means sacking people...laden the company with debt borrowed from the bank...to be paid back...the takeover team will take out their fees...usually in millions...the dis-membered company if it remains intact will have a huge debt mountain to sustain...if broken up and sold in pieces...the worker's pay the price in lost jobs or job insecurity.

The reason a company is broken up and sold is the same analogy...if you sell a second-hand car whole it fetches less than ...if you sell the parts.

As the number of Financial centres increases as other countries get into the money laundering business...the latest entrants are Sydney....Dubai...Pakistan. Interesting to note that Dubai and Pakistan were put on the 'grey' list' for money laundering...yet London and New York...the world's leading money laundering centres are not on the 'grey' list...hypocrisy and double standards...the hall mark of 'Western civilizations'...do as we say...not as we do .

The money markets...buyer be beware...you can lose all your money in the shortest time possible

Where banks...governments ...business...trade in financial instruments...money can be accessed easily short or long term. The money markets... are for big players due to the size of transactions...often in millions.

So, banks may borrow money short term to pay customers ...if it has paid out more than money coming in...business or rich investors can lend money for short periods...companies may borrow money to pay suppliers because its customers have yet not paid. The three main trades are:-

- **treasury bills**...government bonds...a safe bet...interest rates are not good...for pension funds they are a good bet
- **fixed rates certificates**...same as government bonds...not as safe
- **bank deposits**...fixed rates bonds...riskier if bank goes broke...as you are only covered for legal amount determined by the government
- **commercial paper**...fixed rate bonds issued by companies...high risk...not for the risk averse...or people with heart problems or high blood pressure

  In the real-world money markets are for big players...the Major banks and financial institutions run by financial centres like the Wall Street and City of London...they are now all linked digitally and often act together despite the distances.

  The combined actions of these financial centres give them immense powers...they can determine the success or failure of an economic policy of a country...the UK was to find this out when it had to exit the EU exchange rate mechanism...when the money markets determined the UK went into the system at too high a price.

- LIBOR rate...this the rate at which banks lend money to each other...to be determined by market forces...however the banks were able to circumvent this by rigging the lending rates...lots of bad publicity in the mainstream media...small fines for the banks...no one sent to jail.

The Banks are too big to fail and too big to jail...they appear to have immunity from criminal activity...hence criminal activities will continue...keep an eye on the financial press for more bad news...get ready to bail out more crooked banks and financial institutions.

(source:dk publishing how money works)

Foreign exchange...not to be confused with foreign people who want to come to your country on boats...planes...trains

Foreign exchange goes by the name of Forex...not to be confused with a well-known condom brand. The 'condom' gives some protection...not so in the Forex market...you are at the mercy of the money markets...no protection at all.

The forex markets daily trading is huge...as people...business...and governments use them to make money or sell money. As an investor you may get a high rate of return for a deposit in another country...you need to convert your currency to that countries currency

People doing business may buy and sell goods in foreign currency...they need to be aware of the exchange rates otherwise a profit can turn in to a loss...people going on holiday will convert their currency for spending.

Migrants working abroad will be sending money back home...money transfer companies will do the conversion using the foreign exchange markets...before transfer

Speculators and people with more money than common sense can gamble on currency differences...if they bet right they can make money...bet wrong and you lose...your money...your mind...your house...your spouse... be ready to turn up at the nearest soup kitchen.

- **Currency pair**...not a married couple but when two currencies are traded
- **spread**...not to be confused with cheese spread...difference between buying and selling a currency
- **leverage**...trading with very little money in your forex account...leverage is not available to you...you cannot trade on wishful thinking
- **stop loss**...instruction to trader to sell once a currency has reached a certain price...this usually means before you go bankrupt
- **margin call**...your broker will tell you more cash is needed in your account...as your account is reaching a low level which can mean financial trouble ahead and no commission for the broker.
  - (source:dk publishing how money works)

Primary markets and secondary markets

The primary market is used for companies to issue new shares or a company looking to 'float'...i.e. go public. Once shares are bought in the primary market...they then can be sold in the secondary market...in London or Wall street...or the Nasdaq and around the world.

- In the secondary market are what are called 'market makers' who buy and sell shares on your behalf...making a profit on the difference
- the third and fourth markets exists for big investors like pension funds...here investors buy and sell to each other rather than the public

In the real world 'market makers' are can also be market movers...people like George Soros have the ability to move the market in a particular way...this does not have to be very large...small movements can involve large volume of money.

Tiger Moto's advice is stock market investment and speculation is for people with lots of money...who understand the risks...have done their research...who are prepared for losses and can live to fight another day.

Also beware of investment companies selling you shares which cannot be traded in the secondary market...i.e. worthless investment. In the UK the selling of 'penny shares' has led to many disappointed investors...make sure you're not going to be the next one.

Predicting the market...makes astrology look good

Knowing how the market will move is very useful knowledge for an investor...there are two main ways that market prediction is analysed:-

- **market fundamentals**....knowing as much as possible of a market sector...company reports...profit analysis...growth forecasts...competitor analysis...and other statistical ratios to determine whether good to invest.
- **Technical analysis**...statistical data used to see if any patterns can be observed...also how other markets around the world respond can be a good indicator.

    In the real world the best way to predict the market ..is 'insider trading'...illegal but rife in the stock market...those who are able get first knowledge can act first and benefit. Once bad news is made public ...too late for investors...they have already lost.

    Remember the World financial centres are 'Gambling institutions' pretending to be something they are not...Real Casinos are rigged...have a low profit margin...rely on volume of money gambled...Wall Street and London and other financial centres work on a much higher margin...your life savings and investments.

    Applying this to the stock market with a lower profit margin ...but a higher volume of money. Very little of the money that goes through the City of London financial centre actually goes into the real economy...about 2% in the UK

Money laundering centres are depriving governments of tax and money stolen from poor countries deterring development

Arbitrage

This is when traders make a profit buying or selling similar goods...priced differently...it can work with shares...and real assets. However, computers now used to find small differences and trade automatically without human intervention...this is known as 'high frequency trading' or 'stupidity gone mad'.

Since many traders use the same or similar software...it has led to computers causing chaos when they all sell or buy. High frequency trading now accounts for 60% stock marketing trading or 'gambling'

In the real-world arbitrage works differently...in the UK the government has hiked the price of cigarettes to a very high level...to discourage people from smoking or smoking less.

This has encouraged more smuggling...there is now a secondary market in smuggled cigarettes...loss of tax to the government...people not smoking less...simply switching to smuggled cigarettes...or now ...vape cigarettes.

Long term capital management lost $4.6 billion betting on market movements and got it wrong...since the 'bet' relied on leverage ...a small initial cash amount plus borrowings. It was bailed out by...you guessed it ...the US taxpayer...so a private company due to gross mis-management gets bailed out by the tax payer....this should apply to other businesses...logic being the US taxpayer can declare himself bankrupt...no more tax payable.

Manipulating the market...good business logic

This goes on all day...every day...this is normal business practice...occasionally someone will get caught...hazards of the job...the way it works is as follows:-

- buying shares to drive down price...to panic the market to sell more shares...price goes down even more
- buying of shares can signal the market that they are a good investment
- short selling...market manipulators use shares given...at a higher price...manipulate the market to bid shares down ...so they can buy them at a lower price
- a large holder of shares can sell them...which lowers price ...and buy them back

In the real-world market manipulation goes on all the time ...problem is hard to prove...LIBOR rigging only came to light because of 'whistle blowers'...people with Ethics and Morals...as with the Panama papers...how the wealthy hide their money from the tax man....in tax havens. Trying putting your salary in a tax haven and watch the inland revenue raid your house

In the UK the inland revenue negotiates with some rich people and large business as to how much tax they would like to pay...so for large corporations and rich people tax is a voluntary obligation...and all legal

Day traders...or daytime gamblers

These are people who trade large volumes of shares in a day often only holding them for only a few minutes or seconds. They look for small differences to capitalize upon before any stock market correction takes place.

They often do not pay full price for shares...hoping to sell them before full payment due...this is 'gambling'...pure and simple...nothing to do with investing long term...the downsides of day trading are:-

- **high risk**...you can lose a lot of money very quickly
- **stress**...you have to monitor the stock market very closely so as not to miss an opportunity...day traders 'burn out' very quickly
- **expense**...each trade has commission attached to it...this can really cut into your profits

- **scalping**...holding shares for a few minutes or seconds...to make a quick profit
- **margin trading**...paying for a small % percentage of share...hoping to sell before full payment due...this is what caused the 1929 stock market...when the crash came people did not have the money to pay the full price...gambling ...pure and simple...should be outlawed...you should only trade in shares you own 100%
- **bid spread**...difference in selling price and bought price...also known as profit or loss...their profit...your loss
  - (source:dk publishing how money works)

Financial institutions or Global parasites

We are talking mainly about Banks...there also non-bank institutions like pension funds...hedge funds…insurance companies and drug cartels. Non-bank institutions do not need a government to lie. ..cheat and steal money from you ...Banks have to be licenced to do the same...legally that is.

- **Insurance companies** work with or often owned by banks...loans from banks often have to be insured
- **commercial banks**...branch of the same bank you keep your money...they lend your money to businesses who often can't pay back the money...dodgy business practices...you the taxpayer is the loser...When Lehman Brothers bank went bankrupt...lost $639 billion mostly shareholders and depositors' money
- **brokerage**...matches finance for both business and lenders
- **investment bank**...involved in IPO'S....mergers and acquisitions...make hefty commissions in dealings
  - (source:dk publishing how money works)

How banks make money...without too much work

Banks make money by charging interest to lenders...and giving interest to savers...obviously they must charge more to lenders.

The cost of money is determined by the central banks...the way banks make money is as follows:-

- **business account charges**...very high for small business
- **overdraft facility**…very high interest charges...the Mafia charge less
- **interest to savers**...very low rates
- **interest on loans given**...very high charges
- **dividends to shareholders**...reasonable…have to keep shareholders happy
- **credit and debit card charges**...very high
- **attract new customers…** with cash handouts and other goodies...people once they open a bank account...usually keep them for life

Investment banks-invest your money without you knowing it

Like normal banks but much riskier in their operations. Their main function is to provide funding to large corporations for expansion ...mergers...or takeovers...they also have a share dealing service for big investors…broken down there three main functions:-

- **funding trade with their own money**?...yes banks have their own money which they can create out of thin air…they act as investors themselves
- **brokerage**...for grown up adults with lots of money and companies run by chimpanzees to match sellers and buyers of shares
- **provide research**...on economic market conditions...on who to best scam... pensions funds...investors…or the public...or all three
- **raising fund** ...or ipo's listing of new companies to the market plus hefty commission...involves sending out glossy brochures to rich investors telling them fortunes lie ahead if they invest in company XYZ
- **Merger and acquisitions**...lots of hefty commissions to be earned while good companies taken over...dis-membered and sold on...with lots of job losses

- **structuring financial products**...same as above...this time the public sold glossy brochures with unlimited riches waiting for them...if they are willing to part with their life savings
- **hedge funds**...run by people with no morals or ethics...money from rich people...to make money from the market under any condition...how to do this is up to the speculators...as these funds are secret...lots of fraud will be taking place... hidden from view
- **Underwriting**...as in Lloyd's of London...who underwrite insurance risk for other insurers...when you insure your house...the insurance company will re-insure with Lloyd's or some on else...you can become a Lloyd's name and earn money...however if the company runs out of cash they will come to you...you have signed an unlimited liability contract...buyer be beware
- **when new shares...** issued on behalf of a company...offers to buy unsold shares...this does not happen very often...usually the opposite... shares often oversubscribed many times over...it all depends on the opening bid price
  - (source:dk publishing how money work)

Brokerage

A broker brings buyers and sellers of shares together...acts like a matrimonial service except the fees are a lot higher. Today with internet brokerage...the traditional role has gone...however Brokers still used in finding best 'prices' for shares and executing them on behalf of investors...they also manage large portfolios for clients...all with hefty commissions.

For brokers the 'spread' is very important...the difference between selling and buying price of shares...the profit margin...also the frequency of trading of shares...known as the 'churn rate'.

- (source:dk publishing how money works)

The Insurance industry ... their risk...your money

The insurance industry is so vital that we seem to forget how important it is...try buying a house without insurance...or if you are a business... by law you must have public liability insurance.

Insurance is needed by all of us...private ...public...business...governments...the industry is huge...works on a very simple principle...collects small amounts of premiums from lots of customers...hopefully pay out less than what is collected in premiums

- **premium**...the amount collected varies with type of risk...in the UK very high for car insurance...due to many false claims...known 'crash for cash'...people deliberately causing accidents...blaming the other party and making a big claim...get a dash cam ...to avoid being scammed
- **excess**...this is the amount the customer has to pay before the insurance company pays...this is usually set by the insurance company...in the UK car excess is around $500...insurance premiums can be adjusted by varying the excess
- **surplus**...the minimum amount of reserves the insurance company must hold to meet liabilities...the rest can be gambled in the money markets
- **profit**...what every insurance company wants...as long as it collects more than they pay out...there in profit
- **loss**...paying out more than taking in money...if this happens insurance companies will do their best to pay out less
- **investment portfolio**...the premiums collected by the company invested
- **investment income**...as above plus bonuses
- **policy**...the insurance contract you sign...without really understanding what you have signed up to ...the truth revealed when you make a claim

    In the real-world Insurance companies are profit maximizing enterprises...in the UK...12 major insurance companies dominate the market...insurance is divided into blocks...commercial and domestic...each insurance company will specialize in each...insurance is all about risk management.

The way this is done a larger insurance provider will have subsidiary insurance companies specializing say in car insurance...house insurance or shop insurance.

By splitting the insurance risk ...it limits their liability...so in a subsidiary was to pay out more than premiums collected...it can file for bankruptcy and pay nothing...the other subsidiaries will not be affected by this loss

This is the same as the Casino model...contrary to belief you cannot beat the Casino...if you are gambling at say a blackjack table...the maximum payout for the table may be $80,000...once that has been reached the table is closed for further business...the rest of the Casino will function as normal

In the UK majority of car insurance...which you must have by law to drive on public roads...is sold on internet websites. The way the 'con' works is:-

- an insurance company will decide the profile of the customer it wants to insure
- they will have data relating to the number of… types of claims and high risk and low risk areas from existing data
- if you are wanting insurance and you are under 25 years...the premiums will be very high...you are considered high risk
- the over 50's premiums are lower...because this group is low risk
- once the customer profile is determined...the insurance company will decide how many insurance policies it wants to sell and how much profit to make
- if a company decides it needs to sell 300,000 polices...it will offer the first 300,000 customers good deals
- once the 300,000 figure is reached then ...the insurance company will raise the premiums substantially...this is to say...we do not want your business...but if you are dumb

enough to pay the high premiums...extra profit for the company plus bonuses for the management

- When insurance companies are questioned...many say they are paying out more money than being collected...the question to ask ...why are they still in business
- because of all the dodgy claims...insurance companies have tightened up the criteria for paying out
- the way this works is if the claim is less than $2000 they will not ask too many questions and will pay out...this is regarded as a small claim by the insurance company
- claims between $2000- $5000...questions will be asked...proof will be needed to verify the claim.
- any claim above $5000 will be thoroughly investigated

With the above information let me give you real world examples. Business friend of mine in the fashion clothing manufacture industry ..suffered a severe loss when the factory they operated from was destroyed in a fire. They put in a claim for over $250,000...the insurance company agreed at first to pay out...the necessary proof and documentation provided

Later however the company decided not to pay...reason given that the customer had lied on the original application form. The 'lie' on the application... for it asked how long the company had been trading ...the customer wrote one year...the insurance company said it is two years...the customer argued the company was set up one year earlier...they did not start trading till the second year...the first year used to set up operation...i.e. buy machinery...stock...fixtures and hire staff etc.

They went to a no win-no claim Lawyer who took on the case...believing the client to be in the right. Any how the Insurance company wrote to the clients Lawyer stating they were going to fight the claim.

The No win No fee Lawyer realising he was up against huge insurance company with its own legal department....decided no win no fee became... we will take the case but you need to pay us upfront fees before we start the legal case...the 'con' in easy instalments:-

- the insurance company wanted their accounts to be scrutinized by the most expensive accountancy firm they could find...the client charged $5000 for a set of accounts a local accountant charges at most $500
- photo copies of documents from Lawyer costing $600...normal costs $100 at most
- Before going to court the Law firm wanted $30,000 from the client upfront... which they did not have
- the client withdrew a legally valid claim due to lack of money
- and the winner is the insurance company saved $250,000...the lawyer who billed them for his time… $15,000
- and the loser the client lost cash sum $15,000+ $250,000 lost claim ..making a grand total of $265,000
- he now drives a taxi for a living and his wife works

Second case

A retail friend of mine decided to sell the business and do something different. He went from retailing to photo processing. He is a smart guy...he did his market research...did the costings...cash flow forecasts...profit and loss statements for the first year.

He paid $100,000 for a photo processing franchise. The franchise from day one started to go wrong...the Franchise manager in charge...printed wrong flyers...equipment did not arrive on time...when it did arrive...no technicians arrived to show how to use the machine…delays...they arrived six weeks later.

The advertising and promotions did not go to plan...the flyers sent out had the wrong address on them...more delays...after six months and no business...the Franchise company ran into financial difficulties...his Franchise Manager had either been sacked or left.

He decided to take the company to court…again approached a no win no fee Lawyer…who initially took his case with a good chance of winning…later however he decided not to take the client's case…reason the company wrote to him…a huge corporation was going to fight the claim…he realised dealing with the legal department of a huge corporation was going to be an uphill struggle

- he now is back to running a shop…his original business

Tiger Moto's suggestion when it comes to insurance claims is:-

- if you suffer a small loss…do not claim …pay for the damage yourself…i rent a property…some time ago it was burgled…each rooms locks broken…to make a claim i would have to pay the 'excess' that is the first $500 of the repair…the repair bill came to $800
- I paid the $800…reason…the claim would cost me $500 and $300 to the insurance company
- by making a claim…my premium will double in the first year of claim…and for the next 5 years it has to be declared on any insurance application form…meaning i will pay more
- if you make three or more claims within a five-year period…you will find it very difficult to get insurance or none at all
- in assessing whether to insure you …the insurance company will look at the number of claims and the amounts
- if you are going to make a claim….make sure it's a big claim

Third case

Someone… i know decided to set up Claims company…where if you have an accident or are injured the company will act on your behalf…on a no win no fee bases. As soon as he started trading he ran into problems. His customer profile was 25% locals and 75% non-locals (immigrant communities…mostly of Asian origin)

Most of the claims were paid out within a short period of time. The non-locals however...every claim came under scrutiny...delays meant unhappy customers...who blamed him...the business went under.

What actually was happening...was Insurance companies know which group of people are most likely to make false claims...in the UK some immigrant communities are considered high risk.

With this information Insurance companies use delaying tactics and further scrutiny…to filter out false claims. Honest people from all communities end up paying higher premiums...bad news for all of us.

Case number 4

One of the most common claims for car accidents is 'whip lash' injuries...reason until lately whip lash injury were very difficult to disprove...hence the large number of claims. How ever the criteria for 'whip lash' claims have been tightened up and medical diagnoses can determine a genuine injury from a fake one.

A taxi driver customer of mine (of Asian origin) applied for whip lash injury in a minor accident he had...the claim was turned down...the no win no fee Lawyer...then demanded his fees...he refused to pay and was sued by the Lawyer.

It is not uncommon for people involved in car accidents to lie about their injuries...to make false statements...to get friends as witnesses to accidents they were never been involved in…and make false statements...to cause accidents so they can blame others and make personal injury claims.

Honest people to protect themselves from such incidents are using 'dash cameras ' in their cars...which records traffic as you drive along.

In some European countries you have to call the Police in case of an accident...they interview the drivers and take statements…assess the scene and apportion blame...this avoids the lying and cheating as in Little Old England.

As I said before it is not a good idea to make minor claims...only when you are seriously affected should you make a big claim...legal of course...no dishonest claims.

Investment companies

Investment companies are for people with lots of money and little time to invest their money wisely...an Investment company will manage and invest for you ...by an appointed fund manager...also known as the 'fun' manager as he plays with your money...i.e. gambles it...called investing

- Fund managers job is to provide capital growth and income for the client
- he will use his 'knowledge'...skills...along with a team of other people to invest where he believes are good opportunities
- the 'fun' manager will invest in a wide number of assets...from property...to commodities ..to shares etc
- the best strategy to spread risk among a large number of assets
- his performance is based on market expectations...if he beats the market he has done well
- fund managers have their own charges...such as admin charges...entry-exist fees...total fund charges ...any other charges they deem necessary

    In the real world the 'fun' managers investment strategy is more 'gambling' than investing. The big issue is fund managers charge between 0.25-3% of the total in charges. This might not seem a lot but if you are managing $billions of dollars...this small charge can be very substantial

    The 'con' is regardless whether the fund makes money or increases or decreases in value...the fee is taken...it might be less or more . So, the fee system can eat into the income of an investor

    Studies show that people not using a fund manager...i.e. passive investment funds do just as well...so 'fun' managers tend to follow market trends ...rather than have unique knowledge of investment...unless insider dealings.

As an investor i pay 0.25% on my stocks and shares portfolio...the fund has gone down by 5% ...the fee is taken regardless of the circumstances. Investment should be considered a long-term strategy around 10 years...it's not a quick 'get rich scheme'...unless you get lucky

(source:dk publishing how money works)

Non-Bank actors

With the tight regulations on banks after the 2008 financial crash. Opportunities for non-bank actors have been created ...the main ones as follows:-

- **credit unions** have been around a long time...people invest a small amount of money among its members over a given time period. Let's say 12 months...and there are 12 members...each invests $1000 per month...each month one person will get $12,000..until all the members get $12,000 and all members complete their payments
- in the UK credit unions by law are not allowed to lend more than a certain amount...this is so that they cannot compete with the Major banks
- **building societies**...pool the savings of customers and lend for mainly house purchases...many of these are mutuals...as a saver you become a shareholder...the 'con' in the UK many building societies have been turned into commercial banks...savers and lenders are no better off...but the shareholders are
- **pawn brokers**...primarily for poor people to 'pawn ' stolen valuables at very interest rates...because banks do not see these people as a viable business proposition
- **specialist lenders**...personal loan companies...loan sharks... local Mafia or drug barons...very high rates of

interests...non-payment can mean a danger to your personal well-being...these lenders are not to be recommended
- over 40% of people will use a non-bank actors in a year...this is a sad reflection on the dire state of the UK economy as people's incomes...failing to meet their basic needs

Government finance...your money...their stupidity

The total money supply in the economy is a measure of economic activity. The government adjusts this supply by tax and spend policies...by taxing you more it makes your poorer...tax you less make you richer and the already rich even wealthier

The various money forms are divided in to 'm' categories

- **money**...this is circulation of cash notes and coins
- **m1**...banks deposits and savings...traveller's cheques...now card payments
- **m2**..longer term savings...money lent overnight...short term 24 hours...deposit accounts
- **m3**...government bonds...long term deposits...fixed rate 1–3-year bonds
- governments will try to manipulate these amounts...by tax and spend policies...by interest rates...bond purchases...the trick is to have the right amount of money circulating in the economy...not to cause inflation or recession...this is more art than science
- you the reader ...want lots of money...and keep some in the bank ..some at home ..and some converted in to gold...real money

Understanding banks assets and liabilities

When you use the bank as a deposit for your money...once you deposit the money...the money becomes the banks...it will lend the amount less the reserves it needs.

So, in effect debtor and creditor is reversed. When a bank makes a loan...it is recorded as an asset...but as a liability to the customer

After banks close...banks balance their books...now electronic...each bank has to settle its transactions with other banks...this may increase or decrease a bank's assets...if the bank falls short of money it borrows overnight to meet its obligations from other banks or the money markets.

Since money now created by banks as debt with interest charges on it...bank credit money accounts for over 90% of the money supply. This means private banks control the country's economy. So, at election time you should not be voting for Politicians...but for private banks as they control the economy through the expansion or contraction of 'credit money' as debt...i.e. vote for the money party

The private bank's ability to create...restrict...expand or 'destroy' money makes them more powerful than any politician or government. The bond market which buys government debt...hence money creation can determine policies of governments...which will be in their interest only.

Now banks do not need your money to lend money...they do this by simply adding some numbers on a computer screen and transferring them to your account.

The bank will send you a letter confirming the loan and tell you it's in your account...they will not tell you it's been transferred from someone else's account...because its new money created by the bank as debt...credited to your account.

Now I want you review the above paragraph to allow the information to sink in slowly. Can you create the clothes you are wearing from nothing...can you create food you eat... from nothing. Bank 'credit creation' is the biggest con trick in history. It relies on confidence that you can spend bank credit money...here is how the con trick works:-

- In the past money was gold and silver...real money...unlike the 'toilet paper' we use today called 'fiat money'
- handling gold and silver had security issues and portability problems
- since most people only needed a small amount for daily use...security became a problem with the reserve money

- Goldsmiths at that time had safes...people began to deposit the surplus gold and silver with the Goldsmiths for safe keeping
- the Goldsmith would issue the customers receipt for the gold amount and value at that time
- Goldsmiths noticed that most people never came to collect the gold
- the receipts customers held would be traded or transferred in transactions
- so, the receipts became paper money we use today
- the Goldsmiths started to print more receipts than actual gold they held...money printing.
- The problem arose when customers all demanded their gold at once...since the goldsmiths did not have enough gold to match the receipts issued...they could not meet their obligations...today we call this a 'bank run'...the Goldsmith's had to run for their lives...today Banks run to the Government for taxpayer bailouts
- The British Empire did later link the £pound sterling to the quantity of gold it held...this worked for over 200 years...world war 1&2 finished the Empire and its 'gold standard'
- the new imperial 'kid' on the block...the US.. also linked the $ dollar to the Gold standard...it worked till the 1970's when Nixon came of the gold standard
- since there is no gold standard...and no limit to how much money you can create...governments... central banks and private banks have gone mad...endless money printing and credit creation
- result is there is more money in circulation than actual goods and services in the world economy

Bank reserves...the joke of the century

In the past in the US and other countries private banks printed their own currencies which could be used locally... deposited or redeemed.

Due to the many banks runs and angry depositors losing their savings...the US central bank was created to regulate bank activity to avoid future bank runs...not done a good job...the 2008 financial crash...highlighted the Central bank's failure....on more than one occasion. The way bank reserve works as taught and in reality are different.

- **Fractional reserve**...this works on the principle that $1000 deposited in the bank 10% or $100 must be kept in reserve...the other $90 loaned...the loan may also be deposited in another bank or used to buy something...the other bank will also keep 10% and loan the rest
- by this simple trick the multiplier effect means the original $1000 can be converted to $10,000...this is the conventional view as taught
- The second view which is more accurate...that banks do not need depositor's money to lend money. They can credit money to an account ...by a simple book keeping entry...bizarre...yes...but true
- this means banks can create their own credit money and transact business
- this means that banks not only can act as intermediaries...and taking deposits and lending out money...but create money and buy or sell assets
- A major bank had been doing this for years and acquiring assets
- they would lend money to businesses ...after the business was established...call in the loan...knowing the business had no means to pay...otherwise they would not have borrowed the money in the first place...and acquire the asset on the cheap
- **example one...** a family that owned and ran a business park...was encouraged to expand their business

- a business park costs around $50 million dollars to build and operate in the UK
- This family firm arranged the loans needed and acquired five business parks valued at $300 million dollars
- once the business parks were up and running...the bank called in the loans and acquired assets of $300 million dollars for a lot less
- banks can own assets in their own right
- try printing your own money and try to spend or acquire assets with it...not possible...but banks are allowed to do this ...why...because they are more powerful than governments
- **example two**...a company had an overdraft facility of $300,000 which it used for daily transactions (not all the money used...most of the time)
- this facility was withdrawn without notice or reason...the firm could not fund the gap...it went under and sold for a nominal sum...acquired by probably... the same bank by its 'assets acquisition branch'

Recession...depression and your money

The flow of money...amount of money and the velocity of money in circulation is the heart of an economy...like the heart pumping money to all parts of the economy.

However, problems can arise...known as the 'business cycle or 'boom and bust cycle'. The down turn in the economy usually starts with bad 'financial' or 'economic' news. Business and people in times of uncertainty start saving more and spending less.

Business notices this downturn and puts on hold on any expansion plans and also starts to save more...the banks notice this downturn ...start to lend less or have a higher lending criterion...i.e. may request a higher deposit from a house buyer...or commercial buyer

The negative loop reinforces itself and the economy shrinks...if an economy shrinks by more than two quarters in a row we are in a 'recession...let's look at a recession how it affects you in the real world:-

- around the 1980's the UK and US the governments in charge de-regulated the financial markets...also dropped interest rates
- the banks rapidly increased lending...most of the new money ended up in consumer spending...buy now and pay a lot later
- business also borrowed...in the UK it went into landlordism...as the number of landlords is near three million...a non-productive parasitic managerial class...in to property speculation as people bought properties not to live in but to sell for profit
- In the UK the government allows each person a home which is not taxed...people were buying homes...waiting for the prices to rise and then selling them for a tidy profit...this is called 'flipping'
- the UK government has been encouraging house buying with subsidies...taxpayer's money...some of these subsidies have ended with landlords to buy more properties
- the government's aim of house ownership ...has declined for people and increased for landlords...opposite of what was intended
- the UK now has among the highest property prices in Europe...high rents...future generations priced out of the market...house prices in the London Area over valued by 40% in the Northern parts by 30%
- the 2008 crash showed the fundamental weakness of the reckless lending by banks...bailed out by the taxpayer
- the UK economy put under an austerity plan...that is recession to you and me
- all the new money caused inflation...interest rates have risen to quell inflation...loans existing and new one's higher payments...more recession for households...the 'cost of living crises' hitting consumers hard

- in order to hide inflation...business have resorted to 'inflation theft' making things smaller and keeping the same price...hoping customers will not notice this 'scam'
- hidden tax rises ...average tax rate now near 50% for most households gone up from 30% in the past...sales tax now 20%
  - (source:dk publishing how money works)

depression is here

When an economy shrinks by more than 5% it is said to be in depression. You can do this exercise yourself...record all your expenses and income at beginning of year and compare the same data at the end of the year...i can guarantee you will be in depression

- the most studied depression after yours is the great depression of 1929...economists are still arguing today who caused it
- in the 1920's the American economy was booming...rising prices of assets such as property and shares...encouraged ordinary voters into buying such assets...with the unlimited get rich schemes to entice the unwary...many people ended up parting with their life savings and borrowing money for investments
- prior to the 1929 crash which gets little mention is the Florida land boom.
- People were speculating on swamp land on the assumption one day it will be turned into a residential and commercial paradise
- people were putting down 10% of the value of the 'swamp' plot often borrowed...hoping to sell at a later date for a higher price...the 'greater fool theory' in operation'
- the whole Florida land boom went bust...the banks who financed this boom...simply moved onto the stock market...where people started 'margin 'trading ...buying a stock with part payment...hoping to sell at a higher price before full payment due

- the first people who sold out early profited...later entrants suffered catastrophic losses.
- People lost their savings...homes...businesses...banks went under...unemployment rocketed...international trade collapsed
- the contagion affected the US… called in its foreign loans...European banks went bankrupt
- as stated before people hold on to cash in uncertain times...this is known as a the 'liquidity trap'...where cash is abundant...but not circulating in the economy
- what pulled America out of the recession...was world war two...when France and England decided to have another war with Germany to protect their Empires and destroy German industry which they feared
- the Armaments industry and the 'new deal' put the US economy on the road to recovery
- the US arms industry and the US are addicted to endless wars all over the world...bringing…death...destruction...recession and depression all over the world...ask the Iraqi's...the Afghani's...and the Syrians and now Ukraine is being destroyed.
  - (source:dk publishing how money works)

Managing state finance...how to waste public money

Governments provide public services...such as education...health care...pensions…police...army roads....schools...bail out reckless bankers...fund endless wars...corporate welfare...and line the pockets of big business in so called public-private partnerships...which are simply a legal way for private business to rip off the taxpayer…welcome to little old England.

Governments raise money in a number of ways:-

- **printing money**...governments can print their own money without debt.. if they wish to choose...they choose not to.

- **they borrow** the money from banks ...wealthy people and other financial institutions...by issuing bonds...which banks...buy-sell ...who create money out of thin air...and give it to the government...this is the first con trick
- **second option**... they tax people to death at gun point...as tax is theft...where you have no say how the money is spent...that is up to the lying...cheating...Politicians...who con you into voting for policies which are against your interests...as they represent the interests of big business...who fund them and their parties...not you
- **borrowed money** has to be paid back with interest...the problem is governments rarely repay the capital amount...only the interest...and keep borrowing more ...promising to borrow less next time
- government debt keeps rising...debts transferred to future generations
- as for balancing the budget...i.e. money in equal spending...very few governments are able to achieve this...government has just got bigger...and bigger.
- Like drug addicts...governments are 'tax junkies'...addicted to taxes
- you the tax payer is the victim...you have nowhere to hide...unless you leave the country ...then you become another country's 'tax victim'
- while taxes are rising in most countries the benefit system is slowly being dismantled...in the UK...first by restricting claimant's benefits...then reducing benefits paid out...if you are self-employed you will have a very difficult time receiving any money from the state

Governments and your money

How the government 'con'artists and central bank 'con' artists work together and waste your money for your own good...here's how the con works:-

- governments have obligations to fund public services...corporate welfare and the wars...for democracy and human rights
- these cost money...tax never covers 100% of expenditure
- central banks...use a mixture of interest rates...open market operations...selling government debt...and money printing...also creating government debt
- interest on debt has to be paid...since central bank determine the cost of money...they can keep interest low...so as to pay less on the debt incurred
- problem is with all that money printing and bank credit expansion...creates inflation...the central bank then has to raise interest rates to reduce inflation...but it also increases the interest payment on the debt
- before 1909 in the US there was no central bank...and people had public services...government debt very low..
- now debt is rising...taxes are rising...public services are deteriorating

    public infrastructure like roads and bridges are crumbling in the US and UK...the most free market economies in the world.

Central banks...con artists of the 20th century

The central bank's main function is to underwrite the private banksters...to provide money to them when they ruin the economy...the recent one being the 2008 financial market crash...they also:-

- central banks set the interest rate...this can change the amount of money in circulation
- they can set reserve ratios for banks...this can also affect the amount of money in circulation
- they also have to keep inflation low as determined by governments

By using a combination of strategies as outlined above…the central bank hopes to keep the economy in a stable situation. In the real-world Central banks do not control the money supply...as private banks create over 90% of the money supply in circulation

The money markets play a cat and mouse game with the Central banks...trying to guess what its actions are going to be and take appropriate actions to ensure they are not adversely affected.

The private banks control the central bank...not the other way around...the financial markets will send signals to the central banks...(similar to how the Mafia sends threats) on what it would like ..increase in rates or lowering.

The central bank can choose to ignore this...the money markets will punish the country...George Soros proved this...the UK taxpayer ended paying $billions of dollars propping up the pound.

Since the creation of central banks government debts have simply spiralled out of control…how can this bring stability to a country. In the real-world Central bank role and effectiveness is over stated...no less an authority the economist J.K Galbraith described the operation of central banks as over important...the central bank has a big name...small actions...little effective-ness ...economies run by themselves...no one is in charge.

All Central banks do today…is try to control the money supply by punishing borrowers with high interest rates...printing endless money...which creates inflation...which puts up prices…hence increase in interest rates rises...needed….punishing consumers...increasing the national debt...punishing tax payers...creating mass unemployment…punishing workers…allowing endless property speculation...punishing house buyers.

The government budget...a national joke

Governments need to know how much money is needed for public services. Most governments have annual budget forecast...this tells us the difference between tax collected and money needed...it called the fiscal deficit...to cover this deficit governments can do a number of things:-

- **borrow money** which is what most governments do...put up the national debt plus interest charges...the advantage of this is pain to the tax payer limited
    - Politicians love this 'con'.....however over the long-term accumulating debt plus interest...means a countries day of reckoning will come ...when the money markets decide the country is not 'good' for its debt...ask the Greeks.
- **Government prints its own money...**can lead to hyperinflation if not linked to rise in goods and services...Germany tried this in the past...they turned their national currency into 'toilet paper'...today Zimbabwe is doing the same...with the same results...more toilet paper
- **raise taxes**...most difficult to do...tax payer rebellion...voters tend not to vote for parties that will increase their taxes

    Here are the most important government expenditures:-

- Welfare...pensions...health care...unemployment benefits...this is coming under severe strain...as populations age...fewer workers to pay for future pensions and benefits...raising taxes is a non-starter
- so, governments are doing three things..
- (1)**restrict benefits**...in Little Old England it's hard to access the benefit system
- (2) **gradually dismantle** the welfare system over the long term
- (3) **import migrants**...and destroy the fabric of your society...by importing people with dis-functional social values and crooked mentality...leads to citizens voting for anti-immigrant parties

- **(4) increase indirect taxes** which do not get reflected in your wage packet
- **defence**...we definitely need to increase defence spending for all the wars in the name of democracy and human rights...if tax payers were sent a bill for each conflict...there would no wars

  The US the world's biggest arms spender and 'invader' ...citizens do not get tax bills...what they do not realise these wars are putting up the national debt...much of the US debt is related to its 'war machine'
- **Housing**...this is becoming unaffordable for the younger generation...house price inflation and speculation...leading to boom and bust. Countries where renting is the norm such as Austria and Germany...house price inflation is very low

  With over 80% of bank lending in the UK and US towards house purchases...and house subsidies has distorted the housing market.

  People now see the increase in the value of their house as the main way to get rich...known as the 'wealth factor'

  So, a house in the past was seen as some where you lived...is now seen as a financial asset to be traded like stocks and shares...the problem is the next generation have been priced out...and we are seeing a mass exodus of young people.

  In the UK every person is allowed to have one home ..tax free...let's say some one bought a property for $35,000 in 1970...today that property is worth $700,000 in London

  Let's say you over 40 years...worked and paid with average salary of $25,000..tax of 30% =$7,500 X 40 years =$300,000...lets deduct the tax paid from $700,000 ..means you have made a profit of $400,000 less interest on loan say $50,000...net profit of $350,000

  You have from your house got your tax back...paid of the house loan...and made a profit...from an asset which you have done nothing to increase the value...other than live in it

You do not need to learn anything...acquire any skills...no Degree's or other qualifications needed...no training needed...a low I.Q ...business which has made many people rich from asset inflation.

It gets worst...landlords in the UK will often buy properties...interest only property loans...they are cheaper...the tenant will pay the bank loan...and when prices rise sufficiently...the landlord will sell and make a tidy sum from the 'capital gain'...i.e. asset inflation...and it has made many people rich

Again, to be a landlord...no experience needed...no qualifications needed...no Degree's needed...no training needed...a low I.Q business...all you need is deposit for the property ...borrow the rest.

This is the sad state of the UK economy with nearly 3 million landlords and rising...a way of making money...without knowing anything or doing anything...the UK is finished...economically…politically and socially on this model of economic development.

- **The environment**...we all love to talk about the environment...how to save the environment...while we go shopping which is the cause of it. The capitalist system of production and consumption...is using up the resources of the planet fast...and the earth is used as rubbish dump...toxic waste...pollution...climate change...environmental damage

  So, what do our politician do… invest taxpayers' money in green energy and allow fracking...which damages the environment.

  In the US shale gas ...is very damaging to the environment It's very profitable for the companies.

  The environment issue is used as an excuse to tax us...in the belief we are saving the planet...the planet cannot be saved...it will exist for the next 500 million years...it is the human species we need to save...some people are calling this our last century...we are rapidly approaching the 'point of no return' when life for most people will become very difficult .

Taxing the already over taxed will not solve the problem...and subsidizing business to be more environmentally friendly will not work...unless we fundamentally change the capitalist mode of production and consumption.

- **Health care**...we are going to grow old and have health problems

    regardless of your age...anyone can be inflicted by illness. The creation of the modern health care system free at the point of use...is a great achievement. However universal health care system is coming under strain in rich countries...as the population ages...and low birth rates...either...taxes have to rise...care has to be rationed...or import more people into your country and tax them.

    All the above options are difficult for politicians...in little old England the solution...is to starve the health care system of proper funding...the system becomes inefficient...use this excuse to privatize some or all of its services ...under the slogan 'you're better off in the private sector'.

    Those who can afford treatment and cannot wait...will pay...those who cannot simply have to wait. Medical staff are leaving the profession at an alarming rate...what does little old England do...rather than address the issue of pay and conditions...imports medical staff from other countries...Doctors from India...nurses from the Philippines...and describes this as a success story...more like desperation...and your taxes keep rising.

- **Education**...we all need to able to read and write...the US spends more money per child than most other rich countries...yet turns out the least educated children according to international standards.

The education budget is huge ...the people who do not have children resent paying taxes for those who do have children.

Despite your taxes...the education system is not turning out young people with good skills...education and training needed to succeed in the real world...ask any employer and they will vindicate the above

One time boss of the CBI ...confederation of business organization of the UK... Digby Jones was interviewed on a politics show with two politicians on prime-time TV...the Politics show.

He criticized the low educational attainment of school and college leavers...rather than listening to what he said...the politicians blamed each other.

So please keep paying your taxes for an increasingly dumbed down nation...the average I.Q in the UK has been declining for a good number of years...it has not hit 'rock bottom' yet...some way to go.

- **Law and order**...we must fund the Police well ...when people complain about the high taxes and mediocre public services...we need the Police to beat...arrest... and jail the protestors.

- Where ever demonstrations are held...they must be approved...by the police and other governmental bodies...if they believe it will lead to disorder...they can cancel it.

  The cancellation is usually politically motivated...say against wars or Israel or US intervention in some part of the world...or other wars that little old England is involved in...so the Police have been turned into a political tool to be used against the public...as with the miners' strike in the past.

- **Debt and interest**...as the nation's debt keeps rising ...so does the debt and interest payments...politicians promise to reduce the deficit...sounds good...it's a 'con' ...what they mean is they borrow less next time...i.e. reduce the 'deficit'...the problem is the debt keeps rising

Because Politicians make promises with money they do not have for public services we cannot afford...so borrowing keep rising ...despite taxes rising as well...there never seem to be enough tax money...no matter how much you pay...So the annual budget is a big 'con 'job'...more work of art than reality

All that happens the tax burden gets shifted from one group to another...lately from the rich to the poor.

How you are taxed to death

The definition of the state is the 'legitimate use of force'...in practice this means taxing you to death at gun point. The UK code now runs to over 17,000 pages...one of the most complex tax systems in the world.

There are two types of taxes ...direct and indirect. Direct is taken from your wage packet and indirect taxes...or stealth taxes which you may not be aware of in purchase of goods and services.

Taxes in the industrial countries have become a very 'hot' political issue...people rightly believe that they are being 'taxed to death' while they see their public services deteriorating and the welfare system does not keep people above the poverty level.

In little old England surveys have shown they pay the same % percentage of taxes as other Europeans...but get fewer or lower benefits...so the UK taxpayer pays the most and gets least...here are a few varieties of taxes the UK taxpayer is subject to :-

- income tax...national insurance tax..12.5% of income..
- Vat...or sales tax 20% on consumer purchases...not on food
- tax on spirits...wine...beers...tobacco...sweets...crisps...drinks
- airline ticket tax...insurance policy tax…import duties
- petrol tax...climate levy tax...tax on gas and electricity

- capital gains tax...inheritance tax...property tax...business premises tax
- online businesses transactions tax...car tax...corporation tax

  The above is a small number of taxes...you can go to the inland revenue website and download all 17,000 pages of the tax code. The real issue is that the rich and corporations are not paying their share...and governments have made tax friendly legislation...i.e. loop holes for tax to be avoided...as follows:-
- people can set up off shore tax companies and avoid or pay very little UK tax
- for corporations and rich people tax has become 'voluntarily'... some pay less than 3% while for most taxpayers it starts at 20%
- the tax office negotiates with big corporations how much tax they would like to pay...it's true
- $21 trillion hidden in tax havens...many of them run by the British protectorates
- 25% of the world's private wealth in Swiss bank accounts
- $billions in tax not paid by big business and rich people means increased tax for the rest of UK citizens
- non-residential status used by rich people to avoid paying UK tax
- transfer pricing used by companies by shifting expenses and profits from one subsidiary to another
- tax evasion and tax avoidance is rife in the UK...all UK politicians do is call business leaders to committees in the Commons and accuse them of not paying their fair share of tax...forgetting to mention that these very politicians are responsible for business-friendly tax legislation...which enables them to avoid tax !.
- The UK is now seeing a 'brain' drain...as the skilled and educated are leaving in considerable numbers...it is

estimated over five million British people live and work abroad...the highest of any country

Government borrowing in to the future and beyond

Governments have been increasing the national debt at an alarming rate...once the debt exceeds the country's GDP...is in effect bankrupt...this is equivalent your house loan is more than the house value...you can see the problem...this is called negative equity...or bankruptcy.

- The deficit exits in two forms (1) difference between the tax raised and money needed (2) this deficit is in the thinking of politicians who make promises with money they do not have
- every month the 'Central bank con merchants' on behalf of the 'deficit' minded politicians borrow money in the 'bond' market
- the debt has to be paid by present and future taxpayers...the debt keeps rising...with promises from politicians who want to be elected...which means more debt.
- As stated before when the debt reaches a certain % percentage above the GDP of the country...it will be in financial trouble...ask the Greeks...and beware of 'Greeks bearing Gifts'

The Public debt...the tax payer...pays...pays...pays

Always remember taxes were first introduced to fund wars not to help people. In little old England the first 'central bank'...the bank of England was a private bank...function to provide money for the endless wars this country has been involved in.

In the land of the 'free and brave'...the US... 'the rise in national debt spiralled out of control with (1) the Vietnam war (2) the big society programs designed to help the disadvantaged in society...mainly the 'black community'. Wars are expensive...two leading economists in America calculated the Iraq war will cost $5 trillion dollars...they calculated everything from arms supplies...long term benefits to injured soldiers...pensions etc...yet no taxpayer has received the bill for this disastrous war...the cost is accumulation of debt

There are a number of ways governments have in dealing with public debt:-

- lie...tell everything is O.K. ...the debt can be managed as in the US the 'debt' dealing keeps being increased
- print money...something 'central banks 'are expert at'....the increase in money supply will make national debt less in % percentage term...politicians will tell how clever they are in bringing the debt down
- problem if the increase in money supply not matched by increase in supply of goods and services...it creates inflation...and we know inflation is a hidden tax...Germany tried this ...after the world war...it did this to reduce the debt as a % percentage of the GDP...but also destroyed the currency and its purchasing power...i.e. turned the currency into 'toilet paper...' being German...excellent quality 'toilet paper'.
- debt can be internal or external...Japan's debt is mostly internal...while Greece its external...usually it's a mixture of both.

Accountability...making excuses for failure

Most governments every year produce a budget...or income and expenditure plan...it lays out the government's plans for the economy and its priorities. In little old England the annual budget has become an annual circus show...where the media and pundits try to guess what the budget may contain...the public simply wants to know...are we going to be taxed more...or less

The main purpose is to hide the truth of the dire economic circumstances:-

- the existing tax base is simply transferred from one group to another...lately from the rich to the poor
- any tax benefits...amounts to 'robbing peter to pay Paul

- after the chancellor of the exchequer has made his speech in the Commons...the opposition gets to...scrutinize it...lots of laughter on both sides of the house...the only people not laughing...the tax payer who has to pay for it
- the central bank will inform the government of the day...what needs to be done and consequences.
- The politicians will ignore any advice which will be a vote loser...such as taxing the rich and corporations...i.e. the fund managers for the main parties
- the central bank ...prints money...create inflation...raise interest rates...create unemployment...lower interest rates...create a housing boom...prints money...create inflation....and so on ..this has been going on for over 100 years...it has to stop...the people are suffering too much
- the budget is a work of art...conceals more than what it reveals...budgets have little effect on the markets...they already know the limitations in which the central bank and governments work under...i.e. they are broke and need their money
- every year the central bank and the Government will send the 'begging bowel' asking the money markets...can we have some more please'...the begging bowel just gets bigger
- in the UK we have a semi-independent body called the office for 'budget responsibility'...please don't laugh...it is better known as the office for lies and statistics...no one takes their reports seriously...whenever they are reported...it's mostly ridicule
- however, the Central bank has one trick that does work for good or bad...it sets the cost of money...the interest rate...which can affect the economy...but here again can a central go against market expectations.
- The Central bank 'con'... it is given the sole remit to keep inflation below 2.5% ...to the exclusion of.. or above anything else...what this means is that it can destroy the

economy...but as long the inflation rate is below 2.5%...it's a success story.

- The reason as explained earlier is that pensions and benefits are linked to the inflation rate...by keeping the rate low the government saves money
- The biggest 'con' of all in little old England is that in the past pensions were linked to the average wage...depending on years of contributions...some retirees could get up to two third pension of their final salary
- the first 'con' this link has been broken...state pensions are now linked to the 'manipulated ' inflation rate...another 'con job'...the real inflation is rate is twice the stated official rate...it boggles the mind that... people who compile the inflation figures have any credibility

Controlling the economy...a job for the Smart-stupid

Governments try to control the economy by using various tools as follows:-

- **tax**...the more you tax people...less money in their pockets...more for the government to waste on vanity projects ..and wars
- **tax people** less and they will go on a spending binge…cause inflation and personal debt rises
- **increase the interest rates** make everyone suffer...accept savers and investors
- **lower interest rates** and make borrowing cheaper…people will increase consumer spending...more personal debt...create a housing boom and speculation on stocks and shares...i.e. reckless spending on consumption...not production...like starting business
- **Quantitative easing**...money printing or a well-known laxative

    Governments love money ...printing...it's cheap...paper and colour printer is all you need...problem is ...it creates inflation...lowers living standards....and you cannot print you way to prosperity...the Greeks tried it and failed.

- **government revenue**...is what they steal from you in taxes at gun point
- **government expenditure**...is how they spend the stolen money

  always remember the definition of a state is 'the legitimate use of force'...or as i call them the 'tax extortion Mafia'

- **imports**...the stuff we import that we do not make
- **exports**...what other countries buy from us...in the UK we offer money laundering service...the city of London'...citizenships to crooked businessmen...sell weapons to anybody and every body

  The UK also exports many of its skilled...educated and talented people ...who have had enough of the UK

- **foreign exchange**...difference between exports and imports ..in the case of the UK ...country always has a balance of payment problem...imports more than it export...outflow of capital
- **national income** ..the total of government...business...and foreign exchange...in 2015 Japan's gross income was $4.29 trillion...the average Japanese receive very little of this....most goes to big business who own the country...and the government runs the country on their behalf

  Some years ago, someone created an economic model of the economy...based on engineering...by putting inputs ...the system will predict the outputs. This retarded dim wit does not realise that economies are too complex for any one single model.

  National and world economies are like plate tectonics...constantly shifting...the more variables you add to a model the less certain it becomes...however there are a few key indicators which can be used as a guide as to where the economy is heading.

- **Inflation**...lower means a happy consumer...and lower benefits in the UK
- **Growth**...this is the increase in the total goods and services of the economy…..higher growth does not mean you will be better off ...if most of the gains as in the US has gone to the 1%...another way to look at growth is it's the expansion of the money supply and debt
- **unemployment**...a regular occurrence...as a consequence of democracies...electing…amateurs…who have no expertise...other than being politicians...to run and mis-manage the economy
- **wages**...the decline in wages in real terms over the last 30 years…means lowering peoples living standards…higher wages do not translate in to higher living standards if they are lower than the rise in inflation…or cost of living

Economic policy… fact… versus fantasy

Managing the economy is like some Israeli soldiers who suffocate Palestinian children to the point of death...then revive them...the economy works on the same principle how much pain to inflict without killing the host...the big ones are:-

- **Inflation**…as stated earlier inflation is a form of taxation...stealing money from tax payers by stealth...here is how it works

    The government sets a target for inflation...the enforcer the head of the treasury and the central bank governor decide how best to control it

- if inflation too is high...raise interest rates...and taxes...slows the economy by making us poorer
- low inflation...can mean high unemployment...governments spend money...money printing…boosts the economy but increases inflation
- a government needs to work out what level of inflation and unemployment is acceptable...this is determined by their electoral process

- in the UK in the 1990's the property market crashed...while the Conservatives were in power...they paid the price by being out office for 12 years...with new labour in power
- they are determined not to make the same mistake...we have another housing boom in progress...the government is determined to keep the market afloat...despite the fact it's destroying other sectors of the economy
- the small business sector is dying...the young generation are priced out of the housing market...brain drain...as the skilled and educated leave...the property market is kept from crashing by importing massive number of people to the country...this keeps the housing market from collapsing ...by keeping the demand high...and house subsidizes
- overseas buyers and locals speculating on the UK housing market...in and around the London area...there are many empty properties bought by overseas speculators ...waiting to off load them onto the market when prices rise enough...while we have a chronic housing shortage and a homeless problem...and the government is housing refugees in hotels.
- this is the sad reality of how the UK economy is mismanaged...by a country run by...know nothing...do nothing...waste your money...professional politicians
- the Government is unwilling to take actions for fear of losing at the next election...it simply delays taking decisive actions...i.e. kicks the can...down the road'...all that happens the problem gets bigger

Interest rates-something we should all be concerned about

Interest rates are a dangerous thing in the wrong hands...get it wrong you can plunge the economy in to a down turn...in the hands of 'know nothing...do nothing politicians...it's worse than a nuclear weapon.

- Governments like a stable economy where prices do not fluctuate too much...happy consumers...means happy voters

- as stated before the government sets the inflation target...and it's the job of Central bank to achieve this
- the base rate set by the Central bank is the rate at which private banks use and charge their customers...base rate plus what they deem to be good commercial logic
- this in practice means secured loans ...i.e. on an asset such as a house the interest rate is less...and on unsecured loans it higher...with 'loan sharks' it's even higher
- the impact of higher interest rates is...makes borrowing more expensive...reduced consumer demand...higher unemployment...the impact on trade can vary...reduces inflation or (inflation theft as discussed earlier)
- lowering interest rates...means lower borrowings costs...consumer spending rises...consumer debt rises...companies hire more people in an expanding economy...unemployment goes down...value of the money declines...as there is more of it...overall creates a consumer and housing boom...and stock market speculation
- what is the ideal interest is much debated about...my view is 5% base rate is ideal...if inflation kept below 2% percent...these means savers and lenders are not punished

As mentioned the Central bank the 'one trick pony'...low interest rates rapidly expand the economy...accumulation of debt...personal...in land and property and in the commercial sector...reaches a point when the debt burden begins to have a negative effect on the economy...the high inflation rate...remember all that money printing

To bring down the runaway inflation and booming economy ..the central bank puts the brakes on with high interest rates...this is cruel way to cure inflation....by creating unemployment. For over a 100 years Governments have been in charge in Democratic societies...elected to make us prosperous and happy...now you would think this is ample time to get things right.

Since no one is really in charge of the economy...what governments do is conduct economic and social experiments with the public...if they get things right ...they tell you it's because of their stewardship of the economy...if they get things wrong...blame the previous government or external forces...like the Russians or Chinese

As for the role of Central banks they are given too much respectability. The real owners of the country are big business and the private banks who create money as debt and expand the money supply

They also buy government debt in the bond markets....and if they do not like government policy...they have veto power. One time President of the US ...Bill Clinton was to find out. After being elected he was taken by his treasury secretary to meet the 'bond holders' of the major banks...and duly informed they will not lend him the money...for welfare programs he promised the public.

He back tracked on most of his spending commitments....that's how the real-world works. Bill Clinton found out who is in charge of the finances of the country...other leaders be warned take note.

Quantitative easing...the biggest money printing con ever invented

This money printing 'con' took off during the Covid virus epidemic. After shutdown of the economy to the bare minimum...the economy was put on life support with huge cash injections...by printing money in proportions never seen before.

This procedure may has kept the economy alive...the money printing is debt to future tax payers has risen substantially. The rational is as follows:-

- government needs taxes to fund public services and wars
- there are never enough taxes...taxing people more is a vote loser
- the governments new 'con' is money printing or Q..E

- keep interests low...print 'tons' of money ...inject into the economy
- banks will use the new created money for 'productive' parts of the economy
- what actually happens...low interests plus large injections of money...fuel consumer spending plus debt...land and property speculation...the productive parts of the economy see very little of the money
- with more money you get higher prices...hence inflation
- the only good thing about money printing is people do not see a rise in their direct taxes...however the debt incurred will have to be paid...by present and future generations
- the national debt mountain just gets bigger... if you only pay the interest and not capital amount...this is like an 'interest only house loan'.
- however, the day of reckoning is pushed into the future...because no politician wants to tell the public...the country is bankrupt
- One of America's leading economists has calculated that the actual American debt is far higher than publicly stated...i.e. people are being lied to ...nothing new in politics
- the US government alone printed $3.5 trillion dollars...each dollar has an interest payment attached to it.
- So Q.E...quantitative easing (money printing) is the magic bullet...no tax rises in your pay packet...pain less way to steal your wealth...through inflation and money printing...the best government 'con game'...guess who the victim is...you the reader and the general public and tax payer.
- Hymen Minsky...the little read and very important economist...see's the capitalist economy in the West as a pyramid of debt...built over time...until it reaches a point and collapses like a house of cards

- for Minsky...the capitalist system is a very unstable...number of financial crashes since the 20th century would seem to confirm his view

The tax extortion Mafia at work

Regardless of where you live… you will pay some sort of tax...a government cannot exist without taxation…even oil rich countries tax their citizens…very lightly…but they do.

Taxes are an evil necessity which we need to pay for public services...in the UK ...means ...pot holed roads...a Police force more concerned with prosecuting people for online comments...than catching real criminals...a health care system not sustainable...treating anybody and everybody for free...a school system with a low educational standard...funding wars and the 100+ military bases in over 30 countries.

- The best taxes are those...simple to understand...easy to collect...and hard to avoid...property taxes are one such tax...but voter resentment means it cannot be too high
- if taxes are too high ...it will encourage tax evasion and tax avoidance
- if taxes too low public services suffer along with the public who uses them
- sin taxes like on alcohol and cigarettes are already very high. They are meant to get people to drink less...does not work...illicit and smuggled alcohol and cigarettes are rife in the UK...the government loses $millions in taxes
- any tax system should fair and proportionate…those who earn the most must pay the most...not so...simply go on line and find out who pays the least...the rich and corporations...and who pays the most. ..the poor in society...in the UK this is known as a just and fair tax system...and the politicians do nothing ...because they are funded by the rich and corporations

- most taxes are direct taxes...taken from people's wages...others like business and the rich decide at the end of the tax year...how much they would like to pay
- their smart accountants and Lawyers will ensure they pay the least amount possible...by designing 'tax efficient schemes'...with names like how to 'defraud the inland revenue'...taxes avoided...are paid by higher taxes on the rest of us...or reduced public services...in the UK we see both of this
- there is now a renewed call for taxes or higher taxes on things which can be harmful to us...such as too much sugar and fats in foods...alcohol and cigarettes as discussed earlier heavily taxed
- the problem imposing such taxes does not change people's behaviour much...A European country introduced a 'fat tax'...besides being very unpopular...it did little to change behaviour...adverse effect on business with lower demand...leading to unemployment in the industry...it had to cancel it.
- economist Arthur Laffer...constructed a graph showing higher taxes do not mean higher income for the government...for him there is an optimal point where most tax collected...his advice keep taxes low...and more people likely to pay...there is some evidence for this
- taxing things to change behaviour is a very dishonest way for governments to raise revenue...it is far better to educate young people in to sensible eating...drinking...and social habits ...as do the French
- the other issue there many businesses who operate on a cash basis...local trades people in the UK very rarely accept bank transfers or credit cards...in my 30 plus years in business every trade person i have employed will only accept cash
- if you want to pay by credit card or bank transfer...they will charge you more including the sales tax...which in the UK is called Vat...value added tax...the Inland revenue does

have a sense of humour...since when did taxes add any value ?

- The way the inland revenue has dealt with this situation...is to set minimum income from each industry...below which it will not accept...say for taxi drivers it may be $20,000
- in the past people would say they only work part time...this enabled them to access the benefit system...the rules have been tightened up and it's not so easy to claim benefits in the UK
- with the taxi business in the UK ...the road app Uber has changed the nature of the industry...not only do the inland revenue have hard income data...they now know the tax avoided. An investigation done some time ago ...over 80% of taxi drivers were claiming benefits !
- In the fast-food industry...food delivery apps such as hungry house…also now give the inland revenue reliable data...which they have used to assess tax liability...a case where a take away owner under declared his sales...was caught when the inland revenue had access to his food delivery data
- eventually what is going to happen is cash will be eliminated and digital payments will become the norm. China is already doing this ...the mobile phone is used extensively to pay for most things
- on the issue of tax rates...they have been rising in most countries...in the UK the average tax is now nearer 50% ..this means for 1-3 days of the week we work for the government
- the issue of tax is now serious problem ...as we age the pension bill keeps rising...as pensions in most countries paid by those in work...with declining birth rates...new pension payers are in short supply...the pension bill keeps rising as we live longer
- prepare to a be a 'poverty pensioner' in the UK...as the state pension you get… will not be able to live on...for some pensioners winter is a hard time…they have to choose

between 'heating 'and 'eating'...deaths due to hypothermia is common among the old.
- remember the pension scheme is the biggest 'con' game...to get future pension payers...many countries have resorted to mass immigration...it has been pointed out that migrants also grow old
- also, mass migration leads to voter resentment...because it changes the nature of societies and can even destroy the social fabric of society
- the classic example being ghettoization...in the UK in... inner city London 'whites are a minority'...when people mention such things they labelled as racists...which is a good way to create racists
- anyhow the 'racists' have a vote and large numbers have voted for anti-immigrant parties in Europe...on the issue of migration...the migrants coming to Europe would not allow mass migration to their countries...if they were rich and powerful countries.
- The Gulf countries allow migrant labour in to their countries...under strict conditions… not many granted citizenship...or allowed stay once their visa expires
- on the issue of tax ..there is in all countries what is politely referred to as the informal economy...or grey or black economy...this is a part of the economy not taxed
- in Greece around 25% of the economy untaxed...Italy is not far behind...the UK varies between 10-20%..it is very difficult to measure the informal economy...however the supermarkets in the UK...collect data...they say around 80 million plus people resident in the UK
- from this figure it is possible to work out tax collected and tax avoided
- taxes are something you will pay once you reach adulthood...best to be familiar with your countries tax system...and pay the least amount without breaking the law.

Government spending…how they waste your money

When we elect a government it will be based on a party manifesto...which is a work of art...and once in power they are guaranteed to be broken.

Along the usual line we have looked at the state finances and they are a mess...so we have to sort out the financial mess the previous party has left the country in...before we can deliver any goodies we promised you.

The best example of this deceit is when the Conservatives came into power...a politician used the above excuse for over two years...a trained parrot could have done better.

Governments usually inherit spending commitments...the problem is how to pay for them...if the economy declines...most governments have the following public expenditure commitments...i am using the UK as my guide:-

- **health care service**...this budget is only going to get bigger...as we age...we need more health care...as many of us have unhealthy lifestyles...leading to obesity and its associated health problems like diabetes...high blood pressure...drug abuse and alcoholism is another health issue.

    With the physical health problems...there are mental health problems...depression be the big concern...in the UK 1 in 5 people during their lifetime will have mental health problem...remember physical well-being is linked to your mental well-being...healthy body...healthy mind

- **pension and welfare**...this also only going to get bigger...as we age more pensioners...unemployment benefits when the economy is not doing so well

- little old England is solving this problem by having one of the lowest benefits systems in Europe...restrictions on what can be claimed...people's assets...their home sold or a charge put on it for care home services if they end up there...costs between $700-$1000 per week depending how disabled you are...and amount of care needed

- **education**...the US spends more per child yet on international league tables has one of the least educated children...in little old England the smart parents and those can afford it send their children to private schools or have them privately educated.

- The local public schools are more prison camps than schools...unruly behaviour...thuggery...no ethos of learning bullying...racism...uncivilized behaviour.

Schools used as dumping grounds by parents who cannot look after their children properly...or both parents work...after school clubs enable children to stay in school...so children can be picked up by working parents after school hours.

The good schools oversubscribed...which means that a good school in your local area...your child may not be able to go there of right...exams may be needed...so the school picks the child...not the other way around

Consequences are teachers are leaving the profession at an alarming rate...poorly paid profession...difficult to recruit new teachers. If you are bright science graduate...you can get a starting salary from $30,000 upwards...a trainee teacher $20,000

Massive shortage of science and maths teachers...plus the denigration of the profession by successive governments has demoralised the profession...to the point where many are taking early retirement...or becoming supply teachers.

What this means you sign with an agency and you get sent to schools with better pay...paid a better rate per day...often at the school you left. As for the University education...over 500,000 graduate each year...yet there are not enough graduate jobs...with a huge debt for the education to service...many are asking is it worth it.

Many of the Degrees of little or no practical value...useless Degree's...more titles than a valuable qualification for the real world of work. The practical content of average Degree less than 10%...your better of learning something of practical value on Udemy...for less than $100 you can learn a practical skill like video editing

- **Defence**...this must be properly funded for all the wars...especially the US gets involved in for Democracy and human rights...the US has killed more people for these two ideals than any other country in history

The real reason is to keep the military industrial complex in business...funding tax payers' money into the arms industry for threats to its 'national security' that do not exist.

In little old England the armed services are having recruitment problems as people are reluctant to join...do not want to invade foreign countries for the US empire...like Iraq and Afghanistan

The US is addicted to war... the war machine ...keeps raising the military budget ..while the country suffers poor infrastructure...homeless problem and other societal issues which need to be addressed.

Since the military lobby's fund both parties there is agreement on both sides of the political divide we must fund the 'war machine' to the exclusion of other things...as Mark Twain has said...American democracy is the best money can buy.

- **Transport**...roads...rail and communication links are the arteries that connect the country...now you would think proper funding would a necessity. Failure to invest in the US and UK is calculated to cost the economy in $billions of dollars each year.

Poor infrastructure means pot holed roads...congestion...Public transport has been privatised as in the UK...despite this trains still do not run on time...people having to travel longer distances to work...money collected for transport is not well spent...ask any commuter.

- **Interest payments on debt....**this is increasing every year with all that money printing...every month the US and UK government borrows to fund the deficit...the debt adds to the existing debt and only the interest is paid...this interest payment may only be a small % percentage of the tax amount...but the accumulated debt is a very large % percentage of the economy.

  The rational is the debt does not matter as you cannot go bankrupt in your own currency...this logic has enabled the

US to have a debt mountain which gets bigger every year...the US debt now exceeds $30 trillion dollars...that's more than the GDP of the country.

- **Other things**...like the police force...we need to make sure they are well armed...if people complain about being taxed to death...we need to beat them down and arrest them if needed...this is to remind them ...pay your taxes and don't ask any questions...we are becoming a Democratic Fascist State
- **Climate taxes**...another excuse to tax people...while supporting the capitalist system destroying the planet

  To summarise tax rates in the Western world are between 30-50%..Nordic countries and Denmark its higher:-
- you can have high welfare with high taxes...such as the Nordic countries and Denmark
- you cannot have high welfare with low taxes...the US being a classic example
- little old England has tried to have an extensive welfare system like the Europeans and low taxes like the US...we have ended with neither
- little old England has one of the lowest benefit systems...yet our tax rate is higher than the US

Government of the future...we have non

Governments invest in public services we all need such as housing...education...defence...provide a legal frame work...and other infrastructure development and services we need. Before investing governments also need to do a cost-benefit analysis to ensure that public money is well spent.

In the UK there is what is called the public accounts committee which scrutinizes government projects...their findings are quite interesting. Let's have a closer at these investments by using the UK as an example:-

- **transport**...road and rail links are essential...they are the arteries that connect a country. In little old England they are now privatised...on the assumption the private sector does a better job in providing the services

Here is the reality...the UK railway system has been broken up and privatised...and under sold by $1 billion. The rail tracks and trains are separate businesses managed by different companies. Private companies tender for a franchise contract to run specific train lines.

These private companies are still subsidized by the tax payer. The trains run no better than before or the costs have come down much for the average passenger.

It is cheaper to travel from Manchester to London by plane than taking a train at peak hours...even cheaper to take a coach.

Commuter trains are essential for workers to travel to work...they have little choice as public transport cannot do the job

So, the subsidies to the railway companies are a hidden profit for them...as for return on investment for the government is non...a net loss to the tax payer...only Virgin trains have invested in new passenger trains...railway tickets keep rising relentlessly.

Here is how the 'con 'works...imagine you win a franchise contract to run a train line. As a company you will have the contract for a set number of years before renewal...that means you may not be awarded the contract again.

What you do is work out the money invested...return needed...say in 5 years period...so if you invest $300 million and you want a return of 20% which is $60 million per year...for five years $300 million.

You do not invest in new plant and machinery...only what's essential...reason being you will not recoup the additional capital in the time period of the franchise.

You employ the cheapest labour...run the trains on the minimum staff...use technology if possible to replace a manual system and less labour time...employ part time and agency staff who have few or no labour rights...charge what you can get away with...and justify any price increase...use a private advertising and marketing company to lie for you.

At the end of the contract ...if it's not renewed you have made your money and happy shareholders ...at the expense of the UK tax payer...go to website called tax payers alliance...which catalogues all the money wasted by governments on projects and other things

- **Utilities...**gas...water and electricity are necessities we cannot do without...in little old England they have all been privatised with bad results for the consumer...great news for the shareholders...fantastic news for the utility companies...because state monopolies have been turned into private monopolies...return for government…other than the sale of these assets...which were used to bribe the electorate with more handouts to get re-elected...it is a net loss

Here is how the 'con ' works. The utility infrastructure is old and out of date...with water companies the old Victorian water and sewage system needs modernising...the government is broke. Privatization seen as way of dumping the problem on to the private sector and absolve the government of any future liability.

What happened...there are around seven water companies who control the market...there is no choice...you are limited to the company that supplies water in your area…30% of water is lost in leaky pipes before it even arrives to the customers tap. Water bills have doubled…now water meters are being installed...which means larger households bill's will be even higher.

A water company in the South of England needed $billions of dollars to replace the existing water infrastructure...they went to the city of London for finance...they were rejected because the payback period of over 20 years too long for the lenders.

In order to get the funding... the government had to guarantee the loan...with tax payers' money...return on capital for the taxpayer big fat '0'...while the water companies are making huge profits.

What the water companies have done to hide the profits they make is create separate companies...so one company will buy assets such as plant and machinery...another owns the water ways and land...and so on.

By moving costs and profits around these various companies it reduces the profit margins...to make them look like they are charities working for nothing on behalf of the public. The end results...happy shareholders...shares and bonuses for the board members...the loser...the taxpayer and customer.

Also, by using by private contractors...they transfer any liabilities of workers to the private company...i.e. a reduced permanent work force is needed...and off course recruitment of cheap labour...some from overseas.

With the gas and electricity companies the situation is just as bad. The government sold what the 'public' owned to the 'public' in a privatization program. The shares were allocated in such a way that larger institutions like pensions could not buy a majority of the shares.

The intention to create a share owning democracy...the public were offered a maximum number of shares...many people bought them as the number of shares offered were limited and most people could afford the money...not a great amount

The shares were set at a low price...once on the market they reached their true value ...much higher...majority of the share owning democracy sold them for a quick profit...most now owned by institutions like the pension funds...once again gas...water and electricity prices have doubled.

In the UK six companies dominate the gas and electricity market...it is very difficult for new entrants...cost of entry too high...many of the new entrants have gone bust or been bought out. The government has regulators who decide how much gas and electricity prices allowed to be increased by...this is to stop the customers from being 'ripped off'

The way the companies get around the regulator is setting up separate companies... one that buys gas and electricity from the whole sale market...another company sells it to retail customers.

At the retail end the profit margin is around 5%. ..which again makes them look charities...the real profit is made at the whole sale end. And other activities from subsidiaries.

Because of the complex nature of the business model...even the financial times who did an investigation into this model could not come to any definite conclusion...i.e. is the customer being 'ripped off' by the private utility monopolies.

To make things worst...at one time there were around 400 different gas and electricity tariffs to choose from...how is a customer to know what tariff is best...with all this confusion.

Here is how the 'con 'works...a utility company sales person will ring you...he will offer a good deal if you sign up...your gas and electricity bill will be cheaper...once you sign up...for the first three months your bill will be reduced...then the company will do a meter reading and suddenly your bill goes up.

You enquire as to why...will be told your usage has gone up...it's not and you know ...but you cannot do anything now...this is the main 'con' used by utilities companies to get you to switch supplier.

The utility companies are now the most hated along with the politicians who privatized them...and some of them are on the boards of these companies.

To better understand why privatised state monopolies do not work...look the land of the free and brave the US...they had power blackouts in many parts of the country...reason the private companies failed to invest in new infrastructure.

- **Social housing**...we all need some where to live...without shelter you cannot have a decent life. After the second world war...the UK built a large number of social homes at a cheap rent for people on low incomes...they were managed by the local councils...so each council had its own stock of housing which it managed and rented to people in need on a strict criterion.

This system worked because a person on low income who could not pay market rent could get cheap housing from the council...council rents were up to 50% cheaper than private rents

The Conservative government under Margaret Thatcher decided to sell of the social housing to the tenants...the idea to turn the rents in to 'house loans'...i.e. to create a property-owning democracy. The houses were sold with a discount of up to 70% of the market price...dependent on length of tenure. So $billions of public assets sold to the rental 'public' at a huge discount...the results were as follows:-

- some people sold their properties and made a tidy profit...many of these properties bought by landlords
- some people became landlords...moving out and renting their properties at market rents
- some people took out equities from their property...i.e. borrowed money against their house and went on a consumer boom
- the % percentage of owner occupied has gone down considerably... i doubt if 50% are still owner occupied
- and who are the winners and losers...landlords...have now acquired a substantial number of homes ..around 3 million landlords...the residents who got massive discounts on their properties...the loser ..once again the taxpayer who funded it all.

The situation at present ... the UK has the most expensive...decrepit out of date...oldest housing stock in Europe and a massive shortage of affordable homes...and the problem gets worst.

Education for all

We all need to able to read and write...now you would think after around 12 years of schooling people should be competent...wrong...again using the UK education system here is the reality:-

- the budget for education is very large in most rich countries
- in the UK around 25% of school leavers have low grades from their school leaving certificates...they are functionally illiterate
- more people are going to University...but the Degrees are useless...of little practical value...to prove this...science students at MIT were given a few electrical items to assemble and make work

The same items were given at top University in Asia...the result the MIT students could not do it...while the Asian students had no problems.

This high lights how University education is out of touch with the real world. The UK has far more useless Degree's than any other country...it's become an industry

Who benefits from this system...the student gets a useless Degree of little value in the real world plus a life time of debt to pay...employers now have their own way of assessing Degree entrants for jobs...the tax payer loses out as the education system in the UK is not fit for purpose.

With the private sector entering the education system hopefully students have a better choice and more practical based Degree's ...useful and relevant in the real world of work

When it comes to education students and tax payers get poor value for money. The best way to get a better education system is (1) get rid of the educationalists (2) get rid of all the useless Degree's (3) make sure a Degree has 50% practical content...otherwise we get electrical engineering students who cannot wire a plug...Medical students who cannot take blood samples...i have witnessed the above.

Science and Innovation

Governments or should I say the tax payer funds research and development...most off this done through Universities...which are privately run...publicly funded institutions...here is the reality:-

- tax payers' money under the guise of research and development is given Universities and the private sector (known as corporate welfare)
- most of this money brings little benefits to the public...but it does create employment and useless Research Degrees
- the few break throughs in technology...this country is unable to convert the research in to products or services...let me give you two examples
- (1)plastic fittings for connecting pipes in plumbing were invented by a British engineer ...German manufacturers were among the first to realise the potential...they got a head start
- (2) the telescopic ladder was invented in the UK...the inventor had to go to another European country to get it manufactured
- the few success stories get lots of publicity...but reality is different
- Graphene...a technology which allows electricity to travel without generating heat...the discoverer awarded a noble prize...as yet the technology is not mainstream in industry...net loss to the tax payer
- when you buy stuff online the encryption for protecting your payment was invented by two people...(1) British (2)American...today the American guy has a business worth $ millions...while the British guy has got no where

So, who wins and losses from funding innovation and enterprise...Universities and the private sector wins...the people who do the research win...the economy gets a boost

...the loser is the tax payer...as it gets very little in return for the money spent.

Inflation theft

Inflation is the best way for governments to steal money from you. To understand what inflation is imagine an economy with only two apples and two $ dollars...each apple cost $1 dollar...now let's increase the money to $4 dollars but keep the number of apples the same ...the apple now costs $2 dollars.

That is inflation...increase in the money supply without a commensurate increase in goods and services.

Now with all that money printing ...you will get inflation...it's only a matter of time...there two types of inflation...in both cases you the tax payer and consumer pay for it.

- **Cost-push**...when prices of raw materials rise...wages...taxes...unfavourable exchange rate for importers...these costs get transferred in higher prices of goods and services...which leads to inflation
  - **demand -pull**...this is when there is a sudden rise in demand for products and services...i.e. business cannot keep up with demand this can lead to higher prices hence inflation

  -with demand-pull the following factors can affect inflation:-

- **monetary policy**...interest cuts...cheap money and money printing
- **governments** decide to waste your money on vanity projects
- **lowering taxing**...not very likely...but it can mean more money in your pocket to spend on the things you don't need
- **property prices**...the all-time favourite way to create inflation...

  welcome to little old England

- **rapid increase in exports**...unlikely...but can create inflation
- (source:dk publishing how money works)

> The real cause not discussed is the ability of big business to control prices...their buying power enables them to pass on higher costs to customers in higher prices. Yet politicians blame workers demand for higher wages as the cause of inflation
>
> This is backward thinking.... inflation comes first and workers demand higher wages to compensate them for the inflation. Also, the endless money printing by central banks...is one of the causes of inflation...as it devalues the currency...and is form of theft by governments.
>
> Big business hide inflation by making things smaller and keeping the prices the same. Property in the UK is a great way to hide inflation...as a rise in property prices is not reflected when calculating inflation. Regardless who ever causes inflation...it is you the customer that pays for it...so get your wallet out and pay for it.

Balance of payments...how to go bankrupt slowly

This is very simple to explain...hard to understand. Balance of payment is the difference between a country's imports and exports...it is better to have more exports than imports...more money in the bank. However, things get complicated when you breakdown the process:-

- **current account**...is simply the stuff traded between countries...it can be anything...from carrots to cars
- **capital account**...this is simply the movement of money for the stuff traded
- **financial accounts**...this is what each country holds in financial assets…cash...foreign exchange...investments...land...etc
- **balance of payments** is the difference of all of the above

   In the real world using the UK as an example:-

- the country imports more than it sells ...more money flows out than in
- **capital account**...laundered and looted money ..inflows through the city of London...tax evasion by Big business and rich people...money outflows....people selling up and leaving for abroad...or retiring abroad...money outflows
- **financial account**...looted and laundered money...into the UK housing market...crooked businessmen residing in the UK for tax reasons
- **balance of payment**...what this country owes other countries... lots of money for the imports...and 200 years of Colonialism...yet to be paid for
- (source:dk publishing how money works)

Exchange rate fluctuations...for speculators only

Over $5.3 trillion dollars traded on the foreign exchange markets...or forex for short...that's a lot money for speculators. Countries exchange rate is dependent on many factors:-

- the money markets determine the rate of one country against another
- they will look at a number of variable factors...such as political and economic stability...GDP...interest rates...economic policies...inflation...wars...education...future trends
- a weak currency can be due to a number of factors...its credit rating might be downgraded by Moody's or Fitch...low interest rates ...not good for attracting capital...economic or political instability...investor protection may be low...low GDP and growth...high inflation...all these factors lead to a low confidence in the money market
- a strong currency...may be due to ...economic and political stability...high interest rates attract capital...low

inflation...growing economy...all these positive factors make the country attractive...hence high exchange rate

- central banks hold what are known as reserve currencies in other countries banks...these can be used for currency transactions without having to constantly exchange currencies

    - In the real world here is how the 'con' works...the worlds reserve currency is the $ dollar still used in over 60% of international trade.
    - Every central bank need $ dollar reserves...so the Russians will have $ dollar reserves in American banks to facilitate currency transactions. Now these $ dollar reserves belong to the Russian bank...the US has stolen other countries assets...the invasion of Ukraine as an excuse.
    - By doing this... other countries have reduced their $ dollar holdings. The recent rise in the cost of living ..has to some extent must be due to the strengthening of the $ dollar...which is the world's trading currency...against which most exchange rates have gone down.
    - The result of this that other countries need to use more of their currency to buy the same amount of stuff. Pakistan has seen the rupee plunge against the $ dollar which means imports like oil and flour have increased. Speculators also play a role in this...in pushing a currency upwards or downwards...more than would be normal
    - An oil trader interviewed some time ago explained that 60% of increase in oil prices is due to speculators and only 40% due to supply and demand.
    - The exchange markets are not free and fair...and fluctuations in currencies are due to market manipulations and normal factors. That does not

mean that people sit in a room and rig the market...no...big players will take a market position on a currency

- The news filters into the market...encouraging others to do the same ...herd mentality...a country may need to defend its currency by emptying its reserves...once that happens ...the 'money' men move in and extract their profits...from a plunging currency...enabling the 'money men' to buy assets of the country on the 'cheap'.

So, currency traders should not be seen as neutral facilitators of financial transactions...but parasites...that prey on countries...and the tax payers in these countries

The Pension Con

One day we will all retire and hopefully have a pension to live on. The state pensions available to all citizens...who have paid their contribution...in the UK its 35 years...here how the pension scam works:-

- when the pension was introduced in little old England...some people did not live long enough to receive or those who did died early...so funding was not a problem
- as people live longer the pension contributions have not kept pace with the demand...despite the UK having one of the lowest pensions in Europe...in effect a poverty pension which does not meet people's needs
- so, you have the absurd situation that the government pays a pension which does not meet a person's basic needs...that person can apply for additional benefits to top up the pension
- now the sensible thing to do would be to pay a decent pension in the beginning so as not to need a top up...the reason for this is many pensioners do not claim the benefits...either they do not know how to… or too proud to apply.

This is very dishonest and cynical way to defraud pensioners...people who fought in wars for this country...who worked all their lives to build this country...only in their remaining life to live in poverty...the term 'poverty' pensioners are in common use.

- governments in the UK collect tax called national insurance which contributes towards your pension. People in work today pay for those retired...the problem as rich countries age ...there are not enough workers to pay for future pensions...around three working people needed to support one 'poverty pensioner'
- governments have resorted to a number of solutions as follows:-
- raise the retirement age...mine is now to 66 years in the UK
- work longer…i.e. Work till you die...not a good idea....you do not want a 90-year-old plumber...or 70-year-old bricklayer … turn up at your house to do a job and die suddenly...you will have that on your consciousness…and you may be prosecuted for 'working the elderly to death'
- transfer the problem on to the private sector...as happened in the UK where people in pension schemes encouraged to invest in the stock market...with disastrous results
- import lots people to the country and tax them...under the banner...we need more workers ..there is a huge shortage...this is a big lie…the reason there so many vacancies are… they are low paid….pay more and there will no worker shortage.
- Despite importing workers there are still many vacancies
- problem with importing lots of people into your country is people do not like it...they see the nature and fabric of their society altered…and labelling people who object to mass migration as 'racist' is a great way to create 'racists'… as you are not addressing the economic and social concerns of the people.

- one-time Prime Minister Gordon Brown while campaigning was confronted by a pensioner who had concerns about the high immigration in her area...he was heard to remark...that she was a bigoted woman...he paid the price when the comment went viral on mainstream media...it just shows the contempt that our politicians have for ordinary voters and their concerns
- problem with importing more people into your country to pay pensions is...they get old too...this simply means never ending migration to the country...not a good solution
- make people contribute more...raising taxes...when people already are taxed to death...means it becomes a political issue and vote loser
- get rid of the state pension for future generations...this is being considered...young people beware...you may get a letter in the future saying you have to make your own pension arrangements
- have lots of children ...and tax them...as happens in many poor countries...your children are your pension
- get rid of the 2/3 final salary pension scheme...which has now happened for some people
- encourage people to cash out their pension...tax it...and they can invest themselves...people have done this...many buy property and rent it ...they can get more from the rental income than their pension
- continue to lie to the people and say nothing to worry about and use stealth taxes to fund the pension...i.e. tax people to death
- link the pension to inflation and not %percentage of average salary as in other European country...this is big 'con' as the inflation target can be manipulated and the average salary cannot
- the above is how the government defraud pensioners...if the average salary in the UK is £30,000 then the minimum percentage 50% of salary means pension of £15,000 ..in the

UK the state pension is £10600...should be £15,000 ...the government saves or con's pensioners out of £4400

So rich countries are all facing the same problem ..how to pay pensions in the future. Norway and Gulf countries have sovereign wealth funds...Japan invested in the stock market and lost a lot of money.

The UK links it to inflation...import more migrants...work longer...raise the pension age...tax people more. France has just raised its pension age...Germany is doing O.K. for now but its population is ageing…importing more migrants...people voting for anti-migrant's parties...i hope they have plan 'B'

Every country will need to work out how best to pay for pensions...the ideal solution is to pay people enough so that they can save and invest for their own future...low wages and taxing them to 'death' is not the ideal solution…here we confront the core problem of the capitalist system.

The French were on the streets some time ago...they pay up to 50% in tax and are struggling to provide basic needs...you may be next...prepare your banner…with a suitable comment like 'I am bankrupt…been taxed to death

Why governments fail...the new normal

Let me enlighten the reader what a sham democracy is. In the UK every 4-5 years the public gets to vote for a party of their choice plus its manifesto (a work of fiction-not to be trusted).Most of the politicians come from the legal profession...here they are Barristers…in less polite company called something else. The lawyers are very good at winning arguments...that is their profession…to lie for their clients in court.

The only people they convince is themselves...trust in politicians expired a long time ago. So, people tend to vote for the least bad candidate. So, the democratic process boils down to people who know nothing...do nothing...talk too much...and waste public money.

In the real world we do not elect surgeons...but you can be a politician from any background...no experience needed...so we have amateurs running the country and wonder why they are such a disaster.

In Germany there is a Green party member who is in power and is completely 'potty'...she is ideologically driven ..determined to pass polices detrimental to German industry.

In the UK we had Tony Blair...took this country into an illegal war in Iraq on the pretext of a 'dodgy dossier'...stating that Saddam Hussein was capable of delivering lethal chemical weapons in 45 minutes...this cannot be true...it took Saddam Hussein at least 60 minutes to get dressed and have breakfast...the only chemical weapon he made was morning tea

Except those used on the Kurds which the West supplied him with ...when they were happy to sell him weapons of any type...before he became a bad boy !

So, we should not be surprised at government failure...its normal business...there is an old saying in business…you pay peanuts ...you get monkeys...in government you elect lawyers to run the country...you get legislated to death...remember more lawyers...means more laws...which means more lawyers…and more arguments

This is the sad reality of electing people who have no experience or knowledge in the positions they are elected to. You can become Minister for Education...even if you can barely read and write...become Minister for Health...even if you have no knowledge of medicine or health issues.

The counter arguments are that know nothing...do nothing politicians have experts who guide them…this is like saying we will elect a surgeon and a real surgeon will tell him what he needs to do.

So, the big question goes is why governments fail :-

- politicians bribe the electorate with promises that they cannot be met...and the tax payer cannot afford...the first big lie

- once in power you have obligations to meet ...government spending which only keeps rising.
- The choice is borrow more to fill the funding gap or deficit...or tax people more...or a combination of the two...investment from abroad is another option...but who wants to invest in the UK...a rapidly declining country unless you are a crook.
- taxing people directly in their wage packet ..is a guaranteed vote loser...try getting elected by promising to increase taxes
- in the UK the way to tax people is by stealth taxes...the government uses statutory instruments...which means it can raise existing taxes without consultation in parliament...the vat or sales tax is a popular one...when introduced 7% now 20%.
- every Western government elected promises to cut taxes and the size and role of the government...non has succeeded...government just gets bigger…which means more taxes
- lately the magic bullet is money printing to boost the economy…the affects are rising prices...inflation...devaluation of the currency...national debt gets bigger...the debt payments transferred to future generations not yet born
- a country cannot go bankrupt in the traditional sense and write of its debt...there is no international law that allows this…this is the reason third world debt keeps rising...despite the fact these countries cannot pay
- the international lenders who buy government debt take the view that a country will not default on its debt obligations...for the simple reason that future generations of that country will be in debt servitude to the money lenders
- the incompetent and useless politicians responsible will not suffer the day of reckoning...as this event will be long in to

the future when they are not around...or are no longer in politics...thus protected from their own stupidity
- for over 50 years the expansion of the money supply and the boom-and-bust cycle has been with us...the people's suffering goes on

The stupidity of governments has no limit

Albert Einstein defined insanity as doing the same thing and expecting a different result...this also applies to government actions. If money printing gets out of control it can lead not just inflation but hyperinflation...Germany is the best-case study:-

- after Germany was defeated in the first and second world war...a bankrupt country had onerous reparations imposed on it
- it decided to print its way to prosperity and pay reparations...war loans and for public works
- the alternative view is that Germany deliberately printed money to reduce the reparations ...as more money means less debt in relation to the money supply
- regardless which view you like to take...the affect was the collapse of the currency...Germany unable to pay its reparations...invaded by France and Belgium....who occupy the Ruhr valley...take over the coal mines and demand goods instead of money
- workers in the occupied territories go on strike...the government prints more money to keep the payroll going
- as the Germany economy declines...it continues to print money...prices rise...inflation sky rockets
- a new government is installed...prints a new currency...with limits...secured on land and property
- the new currency fixed to the $ dollar ..war reparations and debt cancelled....confidence returns to the German economy

- democracies cannot deal with hyperinflation...it's a vote loser...strong leadership is needed to carry out the unpleasant task of stabilizing the economy...it means taking very unpopular decisions which many governments are not prepared to do ....China and the Gulf countries do not come under such democratic limits...they can do what's needed...and have done so.

Default or die...debt management

Governments like people can get into debt problems...with people.. the issue is personal...with governments the tax payers are made to suffer. Governments need to fund public works and endless wars...remember in Europe even if your country is not directly involved in wars it is supporting one side of the conflict...Ukraine being the latest example.

Governments never seem to have enough money from tax payers....can do a number of things:-

- raise taxes...political suicide...in democracies
- reduce public spending...difficult to do...as it hits the poorest... hardest in society...like pensioners on fixed income....political suicide...has to be done by stealth
- print money...inflation theft...makes everyone poorer...political suicide
- borrow money and pile on the debt for future generations...the painless way...in the short term...price to be paid by future politicians...and tax payers
- like people governments have credit scores ...usually done by two agencies Moody' and Fitch...these days not to be relied on ..it downgraded Russia...one of the world's most resource rich countries
- if you have a good credit rating you are likely to borrow money at a lower rate and better terms and conditions.

    To illustrate how things can go wrong for a country...Argentina is a classic example:-

- Argentina was the richest Latin American country...the phrase to be as rich as an Argentinian was commonly used
- successive money borrowing from internal and external sources...accumulated a large debt which the country was paying interest on
- the 1990's recession however the country defaulted unable to service it loans
- it had to have emergency funding from one of the world's international loan sharks the IMF....or...poverty enhancement programs...cuts in welfare and public spending...selling of public assets...opening the economy to global parasites...who asset strip the country of its natural resources.
- these policies fail to work...brings people onto the streets and riots...further decline of the country ..as lenders frightened of the political instability
- the country borrows more...and pays less...the IMF withdraw funding...more chaos...more people on to the street and riots.
- the IMF program fails...the government is asked to commit political suicide and be voted out office...it only partially implements the IMF 'poverty enhancement program... as I speak...the country has just elected a 'comedian'
- as lenders lose faith and their money ..its credit rating is now junk status...it defaults on the $120 billion owing
- the peso devalues...inflation hits over 40%..unemployment 20%...cost of living crises...more people on the streets and riots.
- people resorted to bartering...or avoid using the peso...it was of little value.
- people try to withdraw savings from bank...the government stops withdrawals...to prevent a bank run...more unhappy people on the streets and riots
- political and economic stability is reached... debt write of... re-scheduling of repayments agreed...the economy starts to

> improve...fewer people on the streets...still unhappy with their government...elect a comedian as their next President

- the comedian is already unpopular...get ready for more people on the streets and riots.
- People...get your banner ready in Argentina...we are being fleeced by the IMF international loan shark
- (Source:dk publishing money works)

To understand how this country has come to this sorry state. Argentina is a Latin American country...a settler colonialist state built on the eradication of the indigenous people...who still exist today in a smaller number...at the bottom of the economic pile.

The descendants of the Spanish invaders...took the best land...control the economic and politics of the country through land holdings and business interests.

Later many immigrants came from Europe after world war one and two...mostly of Italian stock. These people became the majority and the middle class...pushing the local indigenous people even further down the economic pile.

The country is blessed with natural resources...agriculture and beef exports very important for the country...an educated work force...very little industry for export earnings.

Failure to make the rich and business elite pay their fair share of taxes...has meant governments have borrowed to maintain public services...as population increases...demand increases...hence need for more borrowing.

The problem is the majority of the debt has to be paid in $dollars...to earn $ dollars you need export earnings to be paid in $dollars...or you to export to the US.

With the decline of the peso... the $dollar debt rises...which means more peso's needed for each $dollar of debt out of the economy...poverty enhancement for the poor and middle class...hence people on the street and riots.

Since a country cannot file for bankruptcy and write of its debt...it is at the mercy of the lenders...and if the $dollar rises in exchange rate...then the debt servicing gets bigger.

Now the currency traders or parasites also make money from Argentina by devaluing or increasing the value of the currency...as George Soros did with little old England.

There may come a time that Argentina may become like Tanzania which has to borrow the money to pay the interest on loans which it cannot pay.

The best advice is to agree with lenders a fixed amount it can afford to pay...substantial debt write off...or default. As world renowned economist Michael Hudson often says...debt that cannot be paid...will not be paid...he uses financial history to make his argument.

Wealth and income...how to improve your net worth

This is an important chapter as it applies to you...financial planning at an early stage of your life will make for a happy and comfortable retirement.

Planning is simply saving a portion of your income and investing in suitable assets or even starting your own business...if you have to take on debt ...make sure its manageable...use your investment income...when it matures...to reduce debt or increase investment...or you can spend it...if you invest wisely you will have financial independence...and rely on no one.

- **net-worth**...assets less liabilities...a high net worth has $1 million plus in assets...this is your target figure...put in your diary
- **income and wealth**...income is simply money coming in...less outgoings...expenses...what is left is your wealth...for most people today after paying all their expenses...their wealth is a 'tin' of beans in the cup board
- **turning income into wealth**...if you are an employee your income will be fixed...so in order to save more say 10% of your income is a tough task... when you want to spend on so many things advertised that you don't need

    A spreadsheet and a disciplinary approach are needed...decide between essential and non-essential expenditure...then search for the cheapest essentials...in the UK the cheapest grocery supermarket is called Aldi and Lidl or Costco...find a similar one's in your area.

If you are embarrassed at shopping at a discount store then i suggest you use a disguise and hide your face...this might lead to security following you around the store...as long you pay for the stuff...they will not mind

- so, decide how much you can save...stick to a budget...buy cheap...buy what you need...not what you want...shop cheap and invest wisely
- types of incomes...it is better to have many sources of income...small number of incomes can make a substantial amount...say you rent a property. Have stocks and shares...go shoplifting at weekends...you work at care home on weekends helping the elderly how to spend their money ...by stealing it. You deliver drugs in the evening legal and illegal...there are lots of investment opportunities...its best you keep on the right side of the 'law'.
- So, decide between passive and active income...passive is like stocks and shares...active you have to actually do something...a lot harder

So have a portfolio of investments:-

1) property rental

2) shop lifting

3) drug running...high risk ..high reward

4) As financial advisor to your local drug dealer...(high risk high reward)

5) money laundering and loan sharking...high risk...high reward

6) selling stolen stuff on online platforms...low risk...high reward

7) gardening...low risk...low reward...you need to be fit and healthy

- so having a diversified portfolio of investment means you will have income from many sources as above and you will be able to spend your income....most likely in the local prison...if you pursue some of the above options...not recommended.
- Monitoring your investments is important...in the above situation...you need to be aware when the police are going to raid your house
- as discussed the types of investment are ..passive...active...property and business ..each carries its risk factor

  Investment is about risk and return...the old rule is ..do not get involved in things you don't know about:-
- high risk...stocks and shares…gambling in the Stock market casino
- medium risk...property… Renting or buying...risk is a property crash and government interference
- low risk ...savings account at your local bank...as long as the saving rate above inflation rate you are o.k...lately however with rampant inflation...savers are losing out...low risk means low return

The stocks and shares con

Shareholders expect a dividend and capital gains from their shares. Those who bought the over hyped Tesla shares definitely are getting capital gains...as for the dividends...the company is hardly profitable...stock market traders are bidding up the share price which has no relation to any fundamentals...the share price will crash...there will be many losers and a few winners.

As I write this the shareholders have agreed on a pay packet of over $50 billion for Mr Musk…this has no basis in reality to his contribution… simply greed unlimited

Most companies keep shareholders happy by paying dividends above the bank rate. The average shareholder is clueless as to company operations...the Sainsbury supermarket family owners have no interest in the company...most have never been in one of their supermarkets...they simply collect their dividends and lead a good life.

When you hear nonsense about shareholder power...it does not exist...unless you own more than 10% of the company shares ..as Warren Buffet does...he sits on the boards of many companies.

Investment decisions

Most of us want high return and low risk here is the con:-

- savings accounts offer low yield...best left to pensioners who want to supplement their income
- fixed rate bonds are a little better...but you lock your money between 1-3 years...for people who don't need the money straight away...but low risk...good for saving a deposit for a house
- with interest rate savings compounding over a long period is the key...so if you can save for hundred years...a $1000 per month compounded at 10%...you will have a lot of money...the downside you are not going to live that long
- managed funds...for people with too much money...too little ..time to invest themselves...the choice is passive funds which track the stock market index...and active fund where a fund manager (also known as the fun manager)...gambles with your money...he wins either way taking a %percentage of the fund each year
- property rental...easy money...passive income...no knowledge or experience needed... a low I.Q business...everyone does it...my advice do not buy property...unless you intend to live in it

  The rental market has exploded in the UK due to the stupidity of the government in charge. In the UK there are nearly three million landlords or as Marx called them parasites...or as the conservatives call them potential voters...as home owners tend to vote Conservative...renters do not.

The UK has among the highest property prices in Europe. The property model is simple...get a deposit...get an interest only bank loan...get the tenant to pay your bank loan...wait for the coming housing boom...sell the property...make a tidy capital gain. This model has made more millionaires in the UK... than any other business.

The retarded dim wits who run this country have turned somewhere you live into a speculative asset to be traded. You have foreign buyers gambling on the UK housing market...buying property ..leaving them empty...waiting for the next housing boom...the young have been priced out...many contemplating leaving the country...while the UK floods the country with people from abroad...creating an even further housing crisis.

Real business people do not buy domestic property...they may buy commercial property...but most invest in real businesses of providing goods and services in markets with potential for growth and profits.

(Source:dk publishing money works)

Life insurance

Life insurance is essential although many people do not consider when young. There are many types of life assurance:-

- standard life assurance pays out if you die...of natural causes ..illness or death...the con is if you have a prior existing medical condition like high blood pressure...either the premiums will be very high...or the in the event of you dying say in an accident...the life assurance company will blame it on your high blood pressure and not pay

- as you age premiums become very expensive...with pre-existing illnesses almost impossible

- the other type has an investment element...where portion of your premium is invested...hopefully if at the end of the plan you may get all of your premiums back plus a profit...assuming you are still alive

- majority of householders in the UK who have a house purchase loan will have life cover to insure the loan...the lender will insist on this.
- There are many types of covers to suit all circumstances...my advice get the cheapest cover for the maximum amount you can afford...fix them...so premiums stay the same level throughout your life.

(Source:dk publishing money works)

Investing for profit

We all want to be rich or at least comfortably well of... investments are of many types:-

- the traditional investments for most people are...property...stocks and shares...savings...cash
- there are others investments like. Stolen artworks...antiques... ...jewellery...gold...silver...gems... pedigree dogs
- so have a balanced portfolio...of property...stocks and shares... gold...stolen artwork...pedigree dogs...if you are looking for long term appreciation as you age
- the stock market has delivered average 5-10% growth for the last 50 years...which is a great return

Property...how to get rich without knowing anything or doing anything

The property market is now the main way for people to get rich in many parts of the world...especially in the UK. Running a real business takes knowledge...skill...money...and risk in the market place...not many people can do this.

For most people property is seen as a safe bet...but people can lose money from property if they do not understand the property cycle. The obsession with property is destroying the productive base of the economy...it does not generate...many jobs...explosion in debt...best way to bankrupt a country...as Ireland was to find out...when six banks and 40 developers bankrupted the country in a speculative housing boom and bust.

My advice see property as a place to live and invest elsewhere...for those who cannot do anything else here is what you need to know about the housing cycle:-

- **investment in property** is seen as poor man's asset...it enables a person to acquire a high value asset for a small monthly payment over a life time of payments
- **commercial property** is a better investment...it is harder to get a loan...plus initial down payment is much higher...also to consider are business taxes on commercial property
- **property** is either a buyers or sellers' market
- **in a sellers'** market...demand is high...property prices rising...easy to get house loans...low interest rates...construction boom...a speculative housing boom in the making...well come to little old England
- **buyers' market**...slowdown in housing construction...more sellers than buyers...harder to get a house loan...high interest rates...declining house prices

  In the real world there two types of property buyers...landlords (parasites) and house buyers (who want somewhere to live).The UK is a classic example of what happens when you turn somewhere to live into a speculative asset.

  With the sale of public housing...most property is now in the private sector...as a result the private rented sector has exploded...to the point where people cannot afford to buy or rent.

  While at the same time little old England has an open border policy letting in last year over 500,000 people into the country. With on average 500,000 people entering the country every year (despite the manipulated figures)

  The demand for housing and the stress on public services has reached breaking point. London and the surrounding area have the highest property prices in the UK.

London being a money laundering centre…much of the laundered and looted money has gone into the property market…locals have been priced out of the market.

People from London and surrounding areas have been moving to the North of the country and over paying for property which they regard as cheap plus overseas buyers speculating in the UK housing market.

Estate agents now target overseas buyers into the UK housing market. The locals in the North now priced out of the market. I live in Manchester…there new flats being built costing $250,000-$500,000 …locals cannot afford these….they are marketed to overseas buyers…and they are all sold.

Property is a very good way to convert laundered and looted money into a hard asset…not too many questions are asked if you buy property.

The UK property cycle has now reached beyond the 18 years cycle when it should have collapse…the reason it has not has been government subsidies…high demand…overseas buyers…local buyers…landlordism…high immigration.

It is estimated that by 2030 the average house price in the London area will be over $1 million dollars…great news for the owner…problem not many people can afford to buy.

As people leave the London area over 700,000 have already left…there is a labour shortage…lots of jobs…problem people cannot afford to rent or buy in the London area

The Dim wits who run this country and have created this problem…have no solution…reducing house prices is a vote loser. Some councils have their own solution…they decide the percentage of rental to domestic properties…so if a council decides on a 20% rental ratio to 80% domestic…once this figure is reached they issue no more licences for rental properties.

Since the young have been priced out of the housing market...they are moving to cheaper parts of the country or have become digital Nomads...possibly living in another country and working over the internet with employment from their home country...or leaving the country...disastrous for the UK economy.

Another solution by a campaign is called 'priced out'...they suggest property prices linked to rebuild costs...which are less than market prices...so house prices will only rise if the cost of rebuilding rises.

Another vote loser for the political parties...the UK will go the way of Ireland and Spain...once the property market collapses.

So, the policies to increase home ownership...have had the opposite effect...home ownership has gone up...for landlords ...not home owners...there is no law to stop a landlord's from buying as many properties as he wants. So, in the housing market first time buyers are competing with wealthy landlords...and the winner is ……..fill in the blank begins with L and ends with S.

The boom-and-bust cycle is really a speculative property cycle...according to world renowned economist Michael Hudson...the increase in GDP in many countries is accumulation of debt linked to property...not increase in goods and services.

As for the rental property sector in the UK...tax on the capital gains is going to wipe many landlords profit...as has happened in Irland...it has already begun here...worst is yet to come

Home equity release con

Home equity is the difference between the value of your house less the loan owing...so if your house is worth $100,000 less money owing $50,000...equity is $50,000...some people take this out and spend it...i do not suggest you do this ...not a wise investment decision. The home equity scam:-

- there are companies in the UK that provide home equity release schemes
- imagine you are a retiree with a house owned out right...no loan to pay...the home equity loan company will give a %percentage of the house value...usually less than 70%
- you sign over the house to them and become a tenant...once you die they sell or keep the property
- the company will work out the profit it will make from the house...in principle it sounds like a good idea...but there are risks involved
- if you become a tenant in your own home...the equity release company can put up the rent to the point where you cannot afford to pay...and be evicted
- the profit % percentage you pay to the company can-will be very high...the contract will not be in your favour
- my advice avoid these schemes...sell your house move to a smaller property or rent cheap and use the profit you make for spending or investment
- that way you still have a place to live in… or a low affordable rent and money in the bank

Shares...invest if you dare

Most of the shares are owned big investors and wealthy people...the way shares work is as follows:-

- a company can issue shares...or to start-ups...shares are simply capital invested in a business
- when a company first issue shares it gets the money...after the initial offering any shares traded...no money goes to the company ...unless it offers new shares to existing shareholders...not very often...if it does...do not buy ..the company is in trouble
- so, shares are bought and sold on the stock market...a company values may go up or down...it has little effect on the daily workings of the company

- when you buy a share you are looking for the dividend yield… a good profitable company will pay a higher dividend
- however, even if a company does not pay high dividend...it can produce high capital growth...i.e. increase in the value of the share
- as an investor you should look for dividend and capital growth
- The major Financial centres or gambling casino's…making money from selling and buying shares ...to 'investors'...people with too much money and too little knowledge
- today we have high frequency trading where shares are held for seconds or minutes…done by computers
- there is considerable market manipulation...insider trading that goes on...denied by everybody...yet known by everybody working in the stock market
- in the past market traders made money for their investors and earned a commission...today they make money from their investors
- the Commercial bank will tell its wealthy but financially illiterate customer there is a good investment opportunity
- the bank will use its own money plus customers and shareholders and take a market position opposite to what they are telling the client
- once the client and his money part company...the Bank will earn a tidy profit...and the client will lose his money
- this is known wealth by dispossession...the commercial banks and other such investments traders will in effect steal a client's money...legally

In the real world buying shares is of two types..(1) buying and selling shares ..not recommended as an individual you will be pitied against the smartest people in the financial industry.

(2) buy a portfolio of shares either managed or passive or you can be your own fund manager...this is the best strategy...hold the shares for a least 10 years...use the dividends to buy more shares… with the power of compounding...the shares will double within ten years...assuming no stock market crash

- Bull market...when shares are bid up ..market manipulation
- Bear market…when shares bid down…market manipulation

Managed funds-how to make the fund manager rich

These are designed for small investors who have little knowledge or time to invest...most people invest in unit trusts...these are funds that pool small investors money and invest on their behalf...here is how the con works:-

- small investors with even smaller 'brains' invest in unit trusts ..over 2000 in the UK…which are more than the number of companies on the stock exchange
- By making regular payments to the unit trust company...they are given unit trust shares...over time they will increase in value and be given dividends
- in principle unit trusts give small investors access to stock market…but who really makes the money

    In the real-world evidence shows that investing in unit trusts is no better than putting a financial times stock market listing on the wall…and throwing darts and investing in the companies the darts hit.

    Unit trusts have fee 1-3% average of the total fund...so no matter whether the fund goes up or down the fund manager wins. Now you ask why people invest.

    A huge advertising and marketing campaign encourages people with get rich quick schemes... without knowing anything or doing anything...passive investment...now the few success stories of people who do well used to encourage more people into investing.

Again, my advice only invest money you are prepared to lose...the stock market is a Casino...very few winners...lots of losers...buyer beware you may lose all your money...your mind...your house ...your partner...if your investment fails.

(source:dk publishing how money works)

Managing your investment...risk versus rewards

It is said many times to have a diversified portfolio of investment with optimal risks attached...here is what most people invest in :-

- **cash**...savings at a bank...if the interest earned below the inflation rate...watch your money depreciate in value
- **bonds**...fixed rate bonds ..as with government bonds...lately not a good option...with debt spiralling out of control...the bond market may explode
- **shares**...again not for the risk averse...invest what you are prepared to lose
- **property** ...you can be a winner...buy low ...wait for the next property boom...prices are already too high...the property market will burst...it's just a matter of time...government subsidizes and low interest are coming to an end...it is also a political issue
- my advice buy property to live in...and start a business...best way to increase wealth

In the real world if you have lots of money...most likely you will have a fund manager. For those who do not here is some quick advice:-

- don't invest in things you know nothing about
- decide among a diversified portfolio how much you want to invest in % percentage terms and allocate risk to it
- say you invest in the following:-
    bonds 20%... return 10%... risk of losing you money 100%

shares 20% …return 10%... risk of losing you money 100%

property 20% …return 10% …risk of losing you money 100%

- so, by allocating the above you can diversify risk...now using this let's apply this to the real world...your investments:-
- drug dealing 50% return 1000% risk of losing your money 100%
  - money laundering 50% return…1000%..risk of losing your money 100%
- in the real-world high risk equals high reward...my advice stay on the right side of the law

Speculation versus investing

Many people do not know the difference especially those who invest in digital currencies like bitcoin. As an investor it is better to invest in good companies for the long term.

By investing on a monthly basis, you protect yourself from market fluctuations which are feature of markets...wild fluctuations which often have no real evidence for the volatility.

Investing is for people who know nothing and cannot do anything...because if the they did… they would be starting a business or investing in them directly...passive investments mean you are at the mercy of the stock market…the investment funds.. or the companies you invest in directly

Assessing risk...your money…your risk ..their profit

By investing directly or indirectly you are risking your money...there is no risk-free investment. Most people are risk averse...so the investment industry has designed investment funds which in the brochure appear to offer a low-risk investment.

They use past data...charts...financial reports to hide the true high-risk nature of the investment...in small print...difficult to notice...they will say shares can go up or down...a real investment brochure will tell you the following:-

- we have new investment opportunity designed by our marketing team to 'con' you in to investing
- we projected a rate of return above market rate ...our fees will be above market rate and guaranteed unlike your risky investment
- our finance team worked how much we are going to make out of you ..regardless how much you're going to make
- if the investment does well....we will take credit for it and justify our fees
- if the investment does badly ..we will tell you under the extreme economic circumstances...you should be glad you have not lost all your money...we have done our best to ensure this

In the real world there is no such thing as risk free investment. Most people keep their money in the bank ... use it as a safety deposit bank...little do people realise once you give money to the bank it becomes theirs...only a limited amount is insured in case your bank goes bankrupt

When the financial crises of 2008 hit...millions of people all over the world lost their money...or were unable to access it...as limits were placed on withdrawals...there was case of a Russian 'business man' who lost $15 million deposited in a Cyprus bank account...next time i suggest he keep it in a Russian bank or buy gold

Keeping the money at home means risk of theft and it devalues over time if not spent quickly. Gold and silver are good store of value and money...they are small...portable...can be kept in safety box or hidden.

(source:dk publishing how money works)

The ideal portfolio

An economist by the name of Markovitz has designed a mathematical model for the ideal portfolio...here's how it works:-

- the efficient frontier model consists correlating risk and reward to each asset class
- deciding what %percentage of your money to give each asset class
- what is the variability of each asset class
- standard deviation used to determine the volatility of each class over time
- your expected return against your real return ...which will be much lower
- asset correlation as discussed above
- the strategy to re-apportion the asset classes over time to give an overall rate of return

  In the real world ...the economic model and strategy is fine...problem is if everybody uses the model ...then no one will be better off...computerised high frequency led to a meltdown ..when all the computers took the same decisions to sell shares or buy shares...dependent on market expectations as input into the computer program.

Pension and retirement if you can

The pension is by far the biggest 'con' game perpetrated on the public. We are all going to get old and stop working...most of us will rely on a pension to meet our basic needs.

More fraud has been committed in the pension industry depriving people of their fare pension...all legal ..sanctified by governments...here's how the scam works:-

- ideally the earlier you start saving the better the pension
- today there three types of pensions (1)state pension...in the UK...or poverty pension (2) company pension scheme...unless your company goes bankrupt. You will

have a scheme with no money (3) the self-employed...who are at the mercy of the stock market

- as the number of people increases and ageing...the ratio to workers to support those retired has declined...this is with the state pension...which is a giant Ponzi scheme
- company pensions...with a fixed defined pension on retirement only work (1) if the company can afford to do so (2) the company does not go bankrupt...then defined scheme becomes a ...non-payment scheme
- when you get your pension in the UK...you have the option of (1) cash 25% of it and pay no tax...on contributions on which you already paid tax...in effect double taxation
- (2)cash all of it and pay lots of tax
- (3)take the monthly pension and try to live on it...many pensioners take part time jobs to supplement their low pension...there is goes easy retirement plan

In the real-world company pensions have come under considerable financial stress. The company GM motors had a long worker strike all to do with the pension scheme...the company could no longer fund 100% of the original scheme for its workers.

Filing for bankruptcy can mean a company no longer liable or at a much-reduced rate. The retirees of companies are not accepting that they should have reduced pension.

However, in a company the key staff and board members will have gold plated pension schemes...regardless of the company's financial status ...their pensions and benefits are guaranteed...as with a bank which went bankrupt in the UK...the Boss left the company with a very high pension and benefits...the same could not be said of the employees who lost their jobs.

Company pensions are meant to be protected not in the case of the Mirror group where the owner raided the employee pension pot to pay debts...legislation has now been passed to prevent this...time will tell if more. fraud has been committed.

In little old England the new scheme is all businesses with employees must put into a money into pension scheme.

Employer and employee. Some businesses have got around this legislation...by employing people on a self-employed basis...as an example there is well known supermarket in the UK...most of its staff are self-employed...they work in two different branches of the same supermarket. The company pays gross wages...and the employee responsible for tax...national insurance...pension...sickness benefit.

This is a great way for an employer to get rid of any responsibility for the employee...it's profit...profit...for the business. Hence little old England has lots of 'poverty' pensioners... and more to come.

Many pensioners who have taken their pension as a lump sum have been enticed by fraudulent investment schemes with promises of high returns...only to lose all their savings...who are now double poverty pensioners. The government has now set up a pension's advisory service to give pensioners independent advice and how to avoid such scams.

Debt...something we must all get used to

A book called the 'grip of death' i urge all to buy and read. The author makes the point that each generation has to pay more for what the previous generation had to pay for...namely homes. In the past 1970's a house was 3-4 times average person's income...today it 9-14 times that income.

Two biggest assets people buy in their lifetime is a house and a car...most people will fund this with debt after a deposit has been paid.

This is the only way for most people to afford these things. As long as debt is managed there is no issue...when debt is not managed and gets out of control then problems arise for lender and payer...the old debtor versus creditor scenario which has been with us for over 1000 years...to understand debt we must look at history:-

- in the past debt was used to enslave people...debt bondage...and as means of social control
- in little old England there use to be debtors' prisons...or worst you might be sent to Australia...which today would be a good thing...i have been to Australia...it's a wonderful country...they call it the 'lucky country' i agree....its Geography near the world's biggest economy China...it has benefitted greatly...and may it continue to do so
- in ancient times a new ruler would write of the public debt
- today however debt write off is limited to those countries drowning in debt...and as the world-renowned economist Michael Hudson has said many times...debt that cannot be paid ..will not be paid
- today however many countries are drowning in debt...and for people and corporations...debt has become normal part of life...students are well aware of this when they leave University with a useless Degree and a life time of debt
- debt however if used properly can make you rich...as the author of 'rich dad poor dad' says you get rich using other people's money...in his case the Banks... Donald Trump built a fortune on bank lending and bankruptcies
- the stock market gives you leverage...you put a small down payment on a share or other financial asset ..and you sell it before the final payment is due...hoping to make a profit...this is known as margin trading...or gambling.
- if the whole economy is turned into a gambling syndicate then its bad news...as happened before the 1929 market crash
- today we see the same thing with the property sector ...a way of making money without knowing anything or doing anything...i.e. asset inflation

- the process of enticing people starts early...with buy now pay a lot later...initially retailers saw extending credit to their customers as a way of selling high value items
- banks moved in and today they are the main debt providers to people...business and countries
- and here are the tricks banks create money as debt from nothing...let me repeat that banks create 'debt money' from nothing...they do this by simply typing numbers in a computer...a book keeping exercise
- by this process they can create unlimited 'debt money'...the problem arises banks lend long term...difficult to call in loans...if the debtors cannot pay
- money printing is the same...by governments... the process of selling bonds to wealthy people and banks...who create the money as debt...the biggest scam in history and guess who pays for all this debt...you the tax payer...the individual person and business
- the total debt payable now exceeds the GDP of the world...remember when i said we are drowning debt. It's true...US debt hits $30 trillion plus...yet the US economy has not collapsed...for the simple reason you cannot go bankrupt in your own currency
- even the US is now a debtor nation and other countries buys its debt...it's the world's reserve currency ...which gives it a privilege above all other currencies
- it can keep on printing the best 'quality toilet paper' in the world...however there will come a time when people realise it is 'toilet paper' and dump the dollar...that is long way into the future...but the future is near...the BRICS currency will see to that
- so, if you want to be rich ...get lenders and investors to invest in your business or you
- Denmark. A wonderful country which has high tax and high welfare ..a high living standard for its citizens has debt ratio of over 200% to GDP or household income...but

others are not that far behind...how long it can maintain its economic model is to be seen.

(source:dk publishing how money works)

Compound interest ..the eighth wonder of the world...Albert Einstein

In its simple form it is the cost of borrowing money...in its evil form...compound interest works by adding an interest charge to the loan...however the con is interest on the interest is also charged...simple interest is where only interest charged on the loan...no compounding...Compound interest when interest is charged on the interest is the reason for the debt explosion.

By this simple trick if you do not keep up payments the debt rises rapidly. Banks justify charging interest on the interest...as money loses value over time....difficult to comprehend this argument ...you did not lend someone else's money...but created it out of thin air:-

- when the original loan is paid off... the debt money the bank created disappears but they keep your money...what a scam...but banks control the world ...you can see why
- compounding can work for you...its matter of how long you can wait...the longer the time period...the more money accumulated
- compound interest is evil...it is destroying highly indebted countries ...deterring development...keeping countries poor...there should be a debt write off. ..reasons for which I will give later in the next book and solutions to the debt based monetary system.

Loans and loan sharks...how the poor pay more

Loans are usually short term...often with high interest charges. Cash strapped Britons found these payday loans easy to access...small amounts lent at very interest rates...mainly given to poor people...or people with poor credit ratings.

Payday loans come from America...in the UK a payday loan company called Wonga attracted a lot of bad publicity for targeting vulnerable people who were not financially literate.

With rates of near 6000%..it would be cheaper to borrow from the Mafia ...here is how personal loans work:-

- my advice to keep away from them...go to your bank and get a personal loan...they will have you credit history offer a cheaper loan...or borrow of friend or family member
- failing this... credit card companies...unsecured loans if you have a good credit history...dearer than banks ..cheaper than payday loans
- payday lenders and loan sharks (unlicensed lenders) are the scum of the earth...preying on people with little no income...who the main lenders are not interested in
- they charge ridiculous interest rates...not market rates...once people use these lenders very few get out of debt...new legislation has curbed their unscrupulous activities
- in Germany no lender can charge more than 4 times base rate...this is a good idea...the UK must adopt it
- the credit card con works as follows...you buy an item for $100 dollars...payment becomes due...you can pay the minimum...which will be small amount...now let's say you pay $50 dollars...you would expect the credit card company to only charge you interest on the $50 dollars...wrong they charge on the full $100
- it gets worst unsecured loans if not paid back can become secured loans on your assets or wages...there is a sad case of person in the UK...who owed $2000 to the credit card company...was not able to pay back…lost his house worth $32,000 at that time
- in the UK debts of less than $5000…you can be taken to court and possible bankruptcy…very old debtor's laws still in use today...The UK has an out-of-date legal system over 800 years old...not fit for purpose...it needs a radical overhaul

Mortgages or home loans...or the 'grip of death

The word mortgage is French for the 'grip of death' or death pledge. Banks love mortgages or home loans here's how the con works:-

- a person will put down a deposit say 10% of the value of the house lets $10,000 ...borrows the rest $90,000 with a loan from the bank
- he pays a monthly instalment over say 20 years...at the end he will be a happy house owner
- home owners will usually have repayment home loan...the monthly payment will be made up of interest payment and original capital amount…in the early years you will pay more interest...in later years more capital
- endowment mortgages...you pay the interest only and an amount… the endowment which is an investment plan....at the end of the loan period...the endowment or investment will pay of the capital amount.

  Endowments however turned out bad for many people as they did not pay off the full amount ...leaving the householder owing money to the banks. The reason why endowments mortgages were so heavily marketed was they gave high commissions to the seller
- interest only mortgages ...very popular with landlords...they pay a higher deposit...since payments lower...the tenant pays the loan...the landlord hopes to make a profit on the capital gains
- off set mortgages for people with savings...so you only pay interest on the amount owing less the money saved in your account...this was a good bet for my son…

  As i was able to put my savings into his account….reducing the interest payments....he was able to pay a 25 years mortgage in 12 years...many lenders do not offer these any more...as they were not making enough money

- mortgages are of two types (1) variable interest rates (2) fixed interest rates...in the US and Germany they are fixed over the life time of the house loan...in the UK fixed rate is for a short number of years ...then reverts to variable rate
- banks love mortgages...you miss payments they can take your property....until the last payment is made the bank owns the house
- this means that a householder is only one payment away from repossession
- banks make money from mortgages from three sources...the set-up fees ..the interest...and the insurance sold with the house
- the subprime mortgage crises were due to deregulation...reckless lending to people who could not afford to pay...selling the mortgages to other financial institutions like pension funds...in effect the banks became fee agents...not long-term primary lenders
- the result has been tax payer bail out of the private sector...Wall street got bailed out not main street...i.e. the home owners

Credit unions...give credit where its due

Long before banks emerged credit unions existed in many forms all around the world. The concept is very simply let me explain:-

- a credit union is where members get together to save money
- in the community i live in the UK credit unions are quite prevalent...they called 'committees'
- let's say there are 10 members each save $1000 per month...that's $12,000 per month...every month one member gets the $12,000...interest free...done by a lottery
- in the West interest is charged by credit unions as they are more like lenders than savers
- also, in the UK there is a limit placed on how much they can lend...this is less than what banks can lend...the real

reason is that they do not compete with banks...the government gives other reasons to hide the fact of the real reason as above.

- As credit unions are not for profit...banks do not like them...if they become prevalent...they can affect their future profits...which we must protect at all costs...as they run the country by their unlimited money creation as debt

Credit card...buy now pay a lot later

Credit cards if used wisely can be very beneficial...they extend credit...convenience...no need to carry cash...as long as you pay the money by the due date...no penalties or interest is charged.

- The way a credit cards works is the credit card issuer is lending you money to make purchases...i.e. extending credit
- you get better legal protection with a credit card...as the credit issuer is jointly liable in case of dispute of a purchase
- so, if your card was fraudulently used the credit card company can get the money back for you...if you can prove to them you are the innocent party
- those businesses who accept credit card transactions will have signed a contract with strict terms and conditions
- however, you must be warned credit cards for online or general purchases are fine as long as you pay of the balance in full ...they should not used for personal finance...their interest rates are well above bank rates
- the way credit cards make money is from the retailer...charges around 3% per transaction...and from customers who do pay of their full amount by the due date
- they are a good way to build up a good credit history as long as you pay off the full balance
- however, some people lose control of their finances and the interest charges can quickly mount up. ..leading to personal bankruptcy or financial distress

Digital money...the future of money

With online banking...debit and credit cards... the use of cash has been declining. Digital money is already with us...however things are not so simple:-

- digital currency can become universal if widely accepted as a form of payment...like bitcoin
- this is very dangerous for central banks as they cannot control the money supply
- digital currency has many advantages...it can bypass traditional lenders like banks...this is dangerous for banks profits...we must protect the 'banksters' at all costs...so they can ruin the economy at the same time make huge amounts of profits
- digital currency can be used for purchases...peer to peer lending...crowd funding...and other activities...at a very low cost
- central banks are now in the business of creating their own digital currency...which you do not want use...as it gives them control over your money...my advice keep enough money in your bank account for household transactions...and savings in crypto currency...gold and silver...so the government cannot steal your money
- with traditional banking...central banks...prints money...private banks create money as debt...both work together to fleece the customer and tax payer
- money is stored in savings banks...daily transactions by banks...the central bank controls the value of money dependent on how much of it prints
- so, with the present system central bank Mafia and private banks Mafia have full spectrum dominance over the money system
- cryptocurrency works as follows:-

    -it is mined... only a limited number produced each year

-no one controls it ...it's based on a complex maths...difficult

to replicate

-the money is held in a digital wallet...difficult to steal unless

you have the pin codes

-transfers are anonymous...fees very low...transfers instant

-their value increases as more people use them

Cryptocurrency...death of banking

The way bitcoin works is as follows:-

- your bitcoin account is linked to your normal bank
- you buy bitcoins using your traditional bank account...the money is stored in your bitcoin digital wallet...it has all the security to protect your money
- when buying goods and services...you use an online transaction form...a secret key is generated for the transaction...transaction completed using blockchain...which has an audit trail and contains the transaction details
- bitcoin has layers of security...very difficult for hackers to steal your money...or anyone to steal your identity or 'card details'
- however, because of the high security...if you were to lose your security details...very difficult to get your money back
- there is case of a criminal in Germany who has cryptocurrency worth hundreds of thousands of $dollars...the Police cannot access the money ..he refuses to give them the security details

In the real-world cryptocurrency if widely accepted and used is the death of central banking and much of private banking.

Remember when you put your money in the bank…it becomes theirs...the Greek's found out when they were blocked from withdrawing large amounts of money.

With traditional banking the Central bank Mafia and the Private bank Mafia have control over the money system...they can steal your money...they can freeze access to your money or refuse payments…under the new money laundering laws

I use to have a cash machine installed in my retail premise…it was one where I put my own money…the cash withdrawals …would be put into my personal account by the banks.

I would withdraw the money from my bank and fill the cash machine. My bank asked me to come to the bank and explain the money transactions…i.e. why so much money was going through my account. I gave a valid reason and no further action taken…had I not done so …my account would be frozen.

In the US the latest scam is to freeze peoples bank accounts and ask them to 'authenticate 'their personal bank details...i.e. tell us where the money comes…or we will steal your money.

With cash it gets worst. A story in the US a neighbour called the Police because he thought the house was being burgled…the owner away on holiday…the Police arrived...found a large amount of cash in the house and took it.

When the owner arrived and tried to get the money back he encountered considerable difficulties...they ran a business with a high volume of cash transactions…hence why so much cash in the house.

It took them two years fighting in the law courts to get their money back...they were fortunate...others not so. The reason for the confiscation…money laundering laws.

This is interesting if they want to confiscate laundered money then they should raid Wall Street...the world's leading money laundering centre.

Because cryptocurrency cannot be controlled by governments...it will be outlawed...as has been done in China. Crypto currency has the means to facilitate trade at a very low cost...safe and secure to use...with an audit trail...if the law wants to investigate criminality it can provide the evidence.

A retarded dim wit Politician in the UK used the argument that it can be used to launder drug money. She needs to ask HSBC...world leaders in laundering drug money and were prosecuted for it. Any currency can be used for illegal activity...that is not a reason to ban it...on this logic there would be no currency.

My personal view is crypto currency can replace the role of central banks...as it is controlled by no one...and can no market manipulation...here's why it's so dangerous to traditional banks and the central bank mafia:-

- when you send money from one bank account to another...there is transaction gateway which enables this...with international transfers it's the swift system...run by a company in Belgium...but under the control of the US...it can be switched of... as Iran has found out.

  The swift system should be neutral and not subject to political interference. With traditional banks your money is controlled by the Central bank mafia and the private bank mafia...it is subject to political control
- Also, America has stolen the foreign currency reserves of Russia held in its bank accounts used for trade and payments...this is illegal...other countries foreign reserves can also be stolen
- Crypto currency cannot be stolen by the US government unless you give them security details...with a court order
- foreign countries can put their foreign reserves into crypto... it can be used for payments...it cannot be stolen...some

Latin American countries are already using cryptocurrency...San Salvador being one
- the US and its vassal colony the EU will do its best to ban crypto currency or restrict its use...using the money laundering and terrorism argument…or some other feeble excuse
- however, with decline of the $dollar as a reserve currency...and the BRICS countries creating its own digital currency...crypto currency may be able to link to the BRICS currency enabling more countries to bypass the $ dollar...wait and see how things progress

  In the real world banning crypto currency will not work and will have the opposite effect...it will go underground and a shadow banking and trading system will be created…this unlicensed ..unregulated system will be far more dangerous...and will be used for money laundering and terrorism and other legal and illegal activities

  The Central bank Mafia is well aware of the dangers posed by crypto currencies to their business model of endless money printing...so they are creating their own so called digital currency.

  My strong advice… do not put your money into these accounts...better to buy gold and silver and keep at home ...not in the bank vault...otherwise it will be stolen

  So here is the deal for cryptocurrency:-

- imagine you are a trader…and you want buy from another trader in another country...you will convert your money into cryptocurrency and transact the transfer into the other trader's crypto account...which can then be converted in to the local currency of the trader…cost of transaction to you one cent!.
- banks will need to open a crypto account for you...if they refuse or the government bans it...then the whole system goes underground...and banks and governments will lose taxes and profits

- trying to ban crypto is not a viable option...it is here ..it is reality...it can transform societies by liberating them from the tax extortion Mafia... and control of the central bank mafia
- with the rise of the internet as more activity goes online digital currency will become normal...the problem as always who controls it ?..or will it be neutral.
- the cost for business is very low...a great advantage over the traditional banking system...as crypto becomes established it will be interesting how the tax extortion mafia and central bank mafia deal with the issue
  - (source:dk publishing how money works)

Crowd funding

Crowd funding is a great way for charities...start up business and Others to raise money directly from donors...the fees are low...people can donate to... or invest in a business directly...depending on the project and its capital requirement...money can be raised quickly with a world-wide campaign

There are many platforms to choose from ..since no money is needed up front...the platform will take its fees as a %percentage of the total raised. John Pilger the famous journalist was able to raise over $300,000 for his documentary 'the coming war with China'...in six weeks...i being one of the contributors

As yet the industry is small compared to conventional lending ..but is growing ...over time will become more mainstream.

(source:dk publishing how money works)

Peer to peer lending

This is another alternative to bank lending here's how it works:-
- a digital platform that brings people with ideas and no money...with people with money and no ideas together...like a marriage...with a heavy emphasis on the money aspect

- the financial investors called venture capitalists who invest in new businesses...they have a bad reputation as they are now called 'vulture capitalists'...they demand a high stake in the business...their aim to develop the business to sell for a high profit margin
- there also personal investors called 'angels'...these are people often retired business people with money to invest...they can help a new business by bringing their expertise...however not all are 'Angels' in the traditional sense...they can turn into devils ...if they demand too much stake in the business or profits

  My advice keep away from Venture capitalists if you can...be wary of business Angel's...seek the advice of a business lawyer before committing yourself to any business deal. To make this point very clear for you...in the UK there use to be a program called 'Dragons Den'...here how the con works:-

- about four multi-millionaires would sit in chairs while a number of business people would pitch their business plans looking for investment
- the multi-millionaires let's call them 'untrustworthy individuals'...would scrutinize each business project and would offer a proposal for a share of the business for so much money
- the prospective business people would 'negotiate' a share option deal
- most of the time business proposals would be rejected
- the multi-millionaires are given the status of charities helping mankind and the business community.

  The reality of this program is as follows:-

- most of the people looking for money are business who are already successful...most are inventors...who cannot get funding from traditional means for expansion
- they have no choice but to approach alternative funding...hence this program

- the deals on offer are dismal...for a large share of the business they offer a small amount of money and lots of opinions
- if we look at how these people made their money..i am sure we will find many unscrupulous practices
- there is an old saying 'behind any great fortune are hidden crimes
- one of the participants was caught fiddling her expenses...another one accused of being a tax dodger...i am sure the others have no better reputation
- now you ask me how I know this ...here's my story:-

    I use to be a retailer...we had a young chap who supplied peanuts to us. He went one of these programs looking for funding to expand his peanut business...around $400,000. His experience was they were only willing to invest in highly profitable businesses...risk free investment.

    These programs are no longer aired.. as the bad publicity about how they exploit these business people is in the mainstream media.

    Studies of those who were rejected went on to do just as well by getting funding from elsewhere..

    What the program showed to the public how real capitalists work...arrogant...opinionated...full of themselves...no fair dealing...maximum benefit for the least amount of money...the prospective business person...offered a deal worse than the Mafia ...give us most of the business...work for us for a pittance...and you should be grateful for giving you the money.

    These people are sociopaths ...who's moral and ethical values are opposite to the mainstream population...greed unlimited...welcome to capitalism in the 21st century

Under normal circumstances if you offer to buy 20% of the business by investing... your stake should be 20%...not these ..arrogant people who want 80% for giving you 20% or less.

The UK money system

Welcome to the UK the world's leading money laundering centre…are you a Russian Oligarch or some other person looking to invest your laundered and looted money to 'invest'…the City of London is open 24 hours to help you for a fee. We have specialist staff who can help you avoid getting caught by setting up special charitable foundations in tax havens around the world which we control

To understand the real function of the city of London you need a financial history lesson…the story begins…in the beginning:-

- there was the British Empire …built on exploitation and subjugation of people of colour in distant lands
- the Empire came to an end and after the first and second world war…the new imperialist was the US empire…little old England had no choice but allow the US to take over their Colonial criminal enterprise
- a big debate took place in the UK…what are we going to do as we can no longer exploit people in distant lands…and the stuff we make is not good enough for world markets…the US…Germany and Japan make better stuff than we do
- then a bright spark in the 'Times newspaper' wrote an article telling the UK how survive in a changing world
- Turn the country or more precisely 'the City of London' into a financial centre…i.e. a money laundering centre…so we can continue to exploit our ex-colonies by supporting elites and dictators in these countries to steal money on our behalf
- we have a choice of money laundering centres…let's call them franchises. Like then Virgin Islands and Cayman Islands
- these tax havens…are lovely Island nations with more coconuts than people. And more money than businesses

- our overseas money laundering centres scoop up all the illicit...crooked...stolen tax money known as 'flight capital' from poor countries...through our franchise money laundering centres to the City of London ...the world's premier money laundering centre
- we will give the people who steal for us knighthoods and peerages.... British citizenship and full legal protection...so that if the country from which the money is stolen tries to get it back...we will make it as difficult as possible for them

  As Imran Khan found out when he tried to get money back from a businessman...he was told by his legal advisor...not to pursue the case...costs would be more than the amount stolen
- Next... since we cannot exploit people in distant lands...we can bring them to the UK exploit them...to do all the crap jobs for low pay which the locals do not want work for...and rightly so
- the way we will do this is sell mass migration to the population...is to say we are short of workers...and we are now a multi-cultural society
- the migrants will be grateful for coming to the UK...as we have ruined their countries ...impoverished them...deterred development...exploited them
- coming to Little Old England is an opportunity of a life time...and you will spend a lifetime doing a crap job...suffer racial insults...and discrimination...until your children grow up and give you peace and prosperity
- your children will be educated...but they too will suffer racial discrimination...the only way out of this dilemma is to become self-employed...Asians have among the highest self-employment rate
- the few successful migrants will get lots of publicity...to show what a success mass migration and multiculturalism is

- We will not tell the public that we are still an Empire built on looting and exploitation...or the 100 military basis in over 30 countries
- we have to keep up the lie we are a democracy...exploitation and Colonialism and Imperialism does not go well with the young generation...who are well travelled and cosmopolitan in outlook...happy with people of all colours…ethnicity…religions and cultures

If they find out little old England is still an Empire it could be a vote loser. The countries that were subject to British Colonialism know full well what the UK and has done…it will pay for its Colonialism...at some future date.

The City of London financial centre-world's leading money laundering centre

The London stock exchange ...LSE for short not to be confused with the London School of Economics...also known as the LSE...and more respectable.

- The stock exchange lists companies from over 60 countries
- the top 100 are listed on the FT index known as the footsie 100..if you go into business you should aim for this listing...and be in the Times rich list
- next is the ftse 250 of companies...this is the second division with smaller companies
- the ftse 350 is the third division… addition of the both of the above
- next is the ftse small cap ..these are little companies who hope to be big companies some days
- the ftse all share index is the ftse 100 + ftse 250..this is used as a guide how the market is doing for investment purposes
- the alternative market is for even smaller companies...known as the 'junior' market...the aim to give these companies public exposure to raising capital

- (source:dk publishing how money works)

Hedge funds...evil entities

Hedge funds are investments for the rich and other financial institutions. They are purely about making profit not running businesses .They are old style asset strippers.

These are firms who take over companies and sell the company of in parts...this the same as selling your old car as parts ...you get more money...than selling the car whole.

They have been involved in some big take overs off well-known companies...they take over a company with their own and borrowed money...they impose a debt burden on the company...which is their profit and pay back the lenders plus their fees...the company is then disposed of or has to service the debt incurred

The effect is the company is restructured to service the debt rather than service the needs of its customers. The price paid for this is job losses...reduction in the business activity of the business...no new products or services.

In the UK some well-known companies have been taken over by 'hedge funds'...the first thing they do is they do not want unionized workforce...they operate the company on the barest minimum...under the guise of making the company more efficient.

A well-known phone company was taken over from the owner for about $1 billion...the company had a huge debt imposed on it...the new owners took their profit and closed the business...over 5000 people lost their jobs...the price paid for the take over

Some companies to avoid such a fate have what is known as the 'poison pill defence'...a company will take on debt...even when it's in a healthy financial state. The rational is that the debt will discourage a hostile takeover of the company

One day you might work for an evil hedge fund...if you do...you will be sent on a course where any spark of humanity is drained out of you...you will learn to care for no one than yourself...your aim in life will be make as much money as possible regardless of the consequences to society...in effect you will be turned into a sociopath...devoid of any human emotions...compassion or sympathy...and have no family or friends... a small price to pay for being rich and a sociopath

Tax me if you can

A listed company has to be registered and produce annual company report...filed with company's house in the UK.

- It must in a format to UK accounting standards...which are very low...remember a company report is a work of art...the term 'creative accounting' used to produce them...they hide more than what they reveal...never believe what's in an annual report.
- because of all the fraud that has been going on...new laws now can make owners...managers... key employee's...agents of the company such Lawyers and accountants jointly liable for any fraud or other illegal practices
- what this means in reality is if you are an accounting firm and you suspect or know your client is doing dodgy business practices...you by law have to file 'a suspicious activity report' or inform the authorities to investigate...not doing so can lead to the firm being prosecuted
- many accountants and lawyers under such circumstances will dump their client(s)...because if the authorities find out they have crooked client(s)...the authorities will investigate all their clients...something no lawyer or accountant wants...bad for business
- companies also have to pay corporation tax...which for many companies is a 'voluntary' obligation...remember 'creative accounting'...helps in this process

The Bank of England...debt management bank

The bank of England was created in 1694 as a private bank. The deal was Little old England was always in constant wars...the crown needed money for all these wars. The wealthy who had the money ensured that their interests were protected...in effect the crown gave over the control of the money supply to this bank...which is now 'owned' by the government.

- Like Lloyd's of London which is the insurer of last resort...the Bank of England is the lender of last resort to the 'crooked' private banks who brought the world financial system to its knees.
- what this means is that 'crooked' banks and reckless lending...the bank of England will use tax payer's money created as debt to bail them out...then give them stern lectures not to do it again...otherwise we will have to bail you out again
- unlike other insurance companies if you make more than a few claims...your premiums will go up substantially or no one will insure you...because you are a bad risk
- the banks know they are risk free...they can do the same thing again and the bank of England...i.e. you the tax payer gets the bill...higher premiums...more tax debt enforced on you...for the banks its...win-win
- the Central bank's main priority is stable prices...stable currency...control the money supply...interest rate manipulation...low inflation...printing money as debt...and bailing out 'crooked' banks...at tax payer's expense
- the bank also acts as a business buying and selling foreign currency...buying assets...also having a 'gold 'reserve which has been sold off ..so the UK £pound has no gold reserves to back it...not to worry little old England has stolen Venezuela's gold reserves...we can use theirs to back the £ pound...perhaps we can rename the currency the Bolivar-£pound
- the bank of England is really 'one trick pony' as said earlier for the government low inflation is a priority...benefits and pensions are linked to it
- the way the bank of England does this is by raising interest rates...creating unemployment to bring inflation down...as

JK Galbraith has said this is a cruel way to bring inflation down

- best way to describe what the bank of England is doing is 'bloodletting'... bleeding the economy...but not to kill the patient...and the patient is you ...Mr job less
- the bank of England has a monetary policy committee which meets regularly consists of people with big brains and small minds ..to determine how much 'bloodletting 'the patient can sustain'
- the council of economic advisors(big brains-small minds) will look at lots of out-of-date statistical data to determine what state the economy is in
- they will also advise how much 'bloodletting is feasible' or blood transfusion...i.e. money printing is needed
- As JK Galbraith has said the role of central banks is over stated...economies run by themselves...central Banks policies can make them better or worst...more art than science

UK tax system...tax extortion Mafia

Taxes are paid by UK citizens to fund public services and endless wars this country gets involved...being the US 'poodle' it will go along with the US whatever it says...the UK is a vassal state of the US empire...it is not an independent country...the ftse 100 companies index over 50% are directly or indirectly owned by the Americans

the UK tax system runs into over 17,000 pages...it is one of the most complicated in the world...a good source of revenue for accountants and Lawyers...who are able to exploit 'loop holes' in the cumbersome system to get their clients to pay non or very little tax.

The sources of taxes of the UK are as follows:-

- income tax and national insurance are the main ones
- the others are...capital gains tax…business rates….council tax...corporation tax...fuel duty…sales tax…misc.

- income tax…starts at 20% which sounds reasonable but if you add national insurance the total income tax 32%...this is the starting point...it goes up with your income...leading to 50% of total income or higher
- business rates are a fixed tax on business premises...calculated by the tax extortion authority...it is not based on ability to pay...has to be paid whether your business makes a profit or not…even if the property is empty

  There is what's called small business relief...lately however with the rise property values…fewer businesses get the relief. The only other organization that makes you pay regardless of your ability to pay is the Mafia...so the UK government behaves like the Mafia

  The Chinese Mafia the 'Triads' who operate in many parts of the world where there is a Chinese diaspora. Their business model is very simple...they give you money to operate a restaurant...you agree to pay them a fixed amount...if you cannot they take over the restaurant

  The UK business rate Mafia operate on the same principle...a shop near me closed down...the owner could not pay the business rates ...he had no income...the business rates mafia now own the property…they will keep it for a certain period

  Then sell it at auction and get their business tax and other fees. Another customer of mine lost his house for not paying local property tax.
- council tax ..as mentioned is a domestic property tax on all occupied and unoccupied properties...mine is now in excess of $2000..it rises by 5% each…prior to the increase we get letter from the local Mayor...saying the council is in financial difficulties ...hence the need for the rise...this letter gets sent out every year...i have never in over 40 years....known for the council not to be in financial distress.

- corporation tax...is now a 'voluntary' tax paid by big business...some paying less than 3%... in Britain it's called a fair tax ..those who earn the most pay the least...and those who earn the least pay the most
- before some readers say the wealthy pay more...this is true in volume not %percentage...if i earn $100,000 per year and pay 10% tax...now let's say my income goes to $200,000 and I pay 10% ...i am paying more but my tax % percentage is the same
- a not so noteworthy politician on TV made the point the rich paid more tax...that is true…what the two-faced liar did not mention was the tax % percentage
- Tax justice website is an excellent source of information of who pays what ..they compile a corporate tax dodger of the year list... which corporations pay the least…one year it was Britain's leading supermarket ...this supermarket decided to take this small independent website to court..

    however, a national newspaper printed the websites article...the Supermarket withdrew the allegation knowing it would have to deal with the legal team of a national newspaper… Always remember corporations are evil.

Taxes till you die

Taxes are something you will have to pay all your life...and you will spend all your life trying to avoid them...this is a battle to the death literally...the UK personal tax is designed tax you till you die… and at the same time offers investment opportunities to avoid tax:-

- all people working have a personal allowance below which no tax is paid...in little old England its around£12,500…anything above this is taxable
- there are tax free investment schemes called ISA'S where the interest-income earned is tax free...the government is encouraging savings ..so you might be able to buy a house...pay off debts...save for retirement

- in essence these saving schemes are a good option for ordinary people...problem is the people who manage them have a management fee...the income earned has to be above inflation and more than the fee combined. If on $100,000 investment you earned 10% that's $10,000..if inflation is 6% and you pay 1% in management fee total is $7000...you have made $3000 of real income

  Not much to live on...it just keeps the value of your money from depreciating...very little in growth income

- as personal taxes get more personal ... politicians come up with more taxes and more reasons to tax you ..the 17,000-page tax code is going to get bigger...my advice move to a low tax country...unless you are an American...regardless which part of the world you live in you have to file a tax return

Mortgages or home loans...or the 'grip of death'

As mentioned before people love to buy houses...and banks love to lend money for houses...a 'match made in heaven and hell'.

- The biggest debt you will incur is the house you will buy...unless you are very rich...or inherit. Or win the lottery...you will incur a lifetime of debt for somewhere to live
- once you are given a bank loan to buy your house you are obligated pay for the term of the contract...20-30 years in the US and UK...up to 50 years in Germany...and 100-year house loans in Japanese
- you miss a couple of payments....you lose your house...you do not own the house until you make the last payment
- alternatively, you can rent as in many parts of Europe where rents are cheaper than home loans
- over 80% of bank lending is towards land and property purchases...this a steady source of income for banks...who create money as debt from nothing...charge the householder...once the house is paid of...the original loan

vanishes and the money you paid in interest become their capital...lent out to some other house buyer

This has to be the biggest 'con 'in history...can you create a table or chair or car from nothing ...banks create 'magic money'...and we never question it...perhaps it's time to question more.

Tax break for the already rich

Governments offers also sorts of incentives for business to invest...tax breaks better known as 'corporate welfare'... is tax payer money or loss of tax for corporations to invest and expand their business empire

- the rational for tax cuts and corporate welfare is that the rich do not have enough money ...to encourage them to earn more we must give them tax handouts
- the same rational is applied to the ordinary people...they have too much money ..so we need to reduce their benefits and welfare to encourage them earn more money
- please do not laugh and fall of your chair...these policies have been used to cut taxes for the rich and cut benefits for the poor

Buy to let versus buy to live

The retarded dim wits who run little old England have applied the free market principle to where it does not work

- if you like the car i am driving...you can buy one...the showroom will have one in stock or will be able to have it manufactured
- however, if i buy a piece of land or a property...you cannot buy that because…land is a fixed supply...and homes are in short supply ..the country does not build enough….the 'green belt' legislation prohibit urban expansion
- there is a saying ...you can build a motorway through the green belt…but not a house

- when you restrict supply and import 500,000 people into the country every year…you have rampant landlordism...the already rich just get richer
- as the young have been priced out of the housing market...they have no option but to rent...since rents are so high they cannot save to buy a property...many of our young are leaving and the 30 plus group are not having children ...lack of space… living in small rental property
- there are people approaching 40 plus...still living in rental property…they will not be able to get a home loan because of their age
- the whole issue is now a political one ...both of the main parties are responsible...their dilemma is any legislation to reduce property prices is a vote loser…and renters do not vote for the Conservatives
- the young tend not to vote…when they are in their thirties...they will and people vote according to their personal circumstances
- the government has given housing subsidies to landlords in rental benefits...to house builders in tax breaks ...to banks to encourage them to lend to first time buyers by guaranteeing their deposits
- all these schemes have simply kept house prices going up
- a landlord is a 'parasite' Karl Marx...property should for living in...not speculation. Chairman Xi of China...the UK has created nearly three million parasites...long live the parasite
- the negative effect on the economy is now being felt as interest rates rise and the easy money is gone...25% of house loan defaults and repossessions are landlord's not keeping up payments...while other landlords own hundreds of properties
- pitting the first-time buyer versus a rich landlord there is only one winner ...the landlord

In many parts of Europe, the issue of housing has become a political issue...there are more renters than landlords

Landlords have more money and can fund pressure groups to represent their interests...the battle has just begun.

By subsidizing housing ...this money could be spent on the productive parts of the economy...encouraging wealth creating businesses... a complete waste of tax payer's money.

Introducing a tax called stamp duty on house purchases or sales has not made any difference to house prices...and the rent subsidy is predicted to hit £70 billion in the future in the UK.

The Pension 'Con' gambling or investing...you choose ...you lose

We all grow old and will need to stop working...need enough to live usually a pension...in the UK the pension has become a political tool...where the government and the private sector try to pass the pension liability onto each other…ultimately you the tax payer will get the final bill

- for the state poverty pension, you need a minimum number of years of contribution...at the moment its 35 years
- if you miss any years of contribution the state does allow you bring your contributions up to date before retirement
- there also company pension schemes...these are usually invested in the stock market…and other assets ...managed by a private company
- private pensions are for the self-employed...again invested in the stock market...lately they have done very badly...meaning that to get a decent pension you need to make large contributions
- with an annuity ...your pension pot is sold on the open market...usually to an insurance company…they will give you a fixed income until you die

- the 'con' is the insurance company take a gamble that you will die before the fund is exhausted ...and they will win ...or you will outlive the fund and the company loses
- in the real world the insurance company rarely lose...otherwise why offer an annuity
- sipps...was away for people to invest for their own pension in financial assets...once invested they monitor their investments and watch their pension disappear by the high fee's that the pension managers charge and bad investments

The pension industry continues to make huge profits at the expense of its contributors...people's pensions rarely are enough to live on...hence so many pensioners take part time jobs...or have top up benefits from the state for a living pension.

SUMMARY

The history of money is a complicated story...we all need money to have a decent living standard. In most of the world we have a money economy...i have only given a superficial understanding of the subject.

The US the world's superpower has now moved to a new form of Imperialism...the control of the international monetary system by the use of $dollar in international trade and also control of the swift system...patents....the IMF...the World Bank...control of Middle East oil.

The Geo-Political shift in power taking place from the West to Asia...affects us all and our economic future. As the West has de-industrialised ...the UK with manufacturing less than 14 % of the economy and consumer spending accounting for over 70% of the economy...i.e. the UK is now primarily service economy

The service economy is a low paying economy...ask any shopworker...if you end up working in the service economy be prepared for low pay...and long hours. Each generations prospects in the UK are less than previous generations...even though they are more educated...your income determines your living standard...incomes for most people have been declining in real terms.

Having more money does not mean you are better off. Studies have shown that there are percentages for the cost of living beyond which people are made poorer. If you pay more than 25% for your rent or home loan...or spend more than 40% on food and basic items...you are being made poorer

By working out how much you spend on utility bills...rent or bank loan...food. Car expenses...and by measuring these against past data...it is possible to work out if people are better or worst of than previous generations.

Current data suggests most people are worst off...the purchasing power of money has been declining...i.e. your money buys you less...the so called 'cost of living crises'

People in order to maintain their living standards have been borrowing...personal debt has exploded since the 80' and 90's...as debt levels reach unsustainable levels...especially since the interest rates have gone up...personal bankruptcies have gone up.

The young who go to University are leaving with low economic prospectives and high debt...add the student loan to their personal debt and a possible home loan...they are debt slaves for most of their lives

The whole idea of Politics...economics and democracies are to set people free from debt and wage slavery...ultimate freedom is financial security...having enough money to live on and being debt free...or having a debt level that does not lower your living standard.

In the real world the opposite has been happening for most people...people's purchasing power has been going down...debt levels going up...wages stagnant...or not rising to compensate for the rise in living costs...with low economic growth ...the situation can only get worst.

Every person needs to have a financial plan of its investments and spending...the problem is people do not have enough money to save or invest because of the high cost of living...the jobs market pays very little above the minimum wage...which is a poverty wage. Now two people in a household have to work to maintain a decent living standard...people are having fewer children...which means fewer workers in the future to pay for pensions of the those who will retire...one day it will be you.

So, we are heading for turbulent times...work out a financial strategy for the future which is unknown...you need savings or access to capital. The best investment you can make is in yourself... by having a trade...profession...qualifications...or skills that are marketable and transferable you have a much better chance of surviving in an increasingly uncertain world.

I live in the UK ..a country which in real terms has been declining Politically and economically. This has been due to bad policies of successive governments. The UK in the past was responsible for 40% of the world's manufactured output...today it is a shell of country. A book called Surrender catalogues the decline of manufacturing in the UK. We are too reliant on the City of London and the low paying service sector.

Today our service sector accounts for 80% of our economy...that is people going shopping. The UK has been turned into a warehouse selling stuff made abroad. Former CEO of ICI...the chemical company use to say that you cannot be a successful economy unless you have manufacturing base...today it is less than 14% of the economy and declining. As a former retailer the service sector is a low margin...high volume...and low paid sector of the economy

The Future of Money

As money is becoming digital and global shift in power is taking place...the future is Asia...we are in the Asian century. You should not be worried...empire's rise and fall...as the US empire is in the decline phase...it is a dangerous time as it tries its best to hold on to power. The hybrid economic war with Russia and China is affecting the economic prospects of all of us.

China and other countries in the BRICS alliance are creating a new trading currency backed by gold and commodities…and the creation of an alternative payment system enabling countries to by-pass the $dollar.

As yet the $dollar is still used in most international transactions…however once the BRICS currency is established countries will be able to buy oil without need for $dollars…this will have a huge effect on the world economy as it will be the beginning of the end of the US $dollar hegemony…be prepared for more wars.

What does this mean for you…lots of opportunities…as the rest of the world develops if you have a trade…skill or profession that a country needs…you will do very well.

Always remember do not simply look at the amount of money you will make…but lifestyle…purchasing power…how much your money buy's goods and services…and other factors. So, you may be better off with a lower income and better lifestyle

Digital money…block chain development and digital currencies such as bitcoin are going to transform the global financial payment systems…as it is work in progress no one is sure what the outcome will be. So be familiar with the latest technology so that you can benefit from it in a rapidly changing world.

As we enter a multi-polar word our relationship to money will also change…digital money will allow you to transact business at a much lower cost…and more secure. If countries were to adopt a digital citizens income poverty can be eliminated so that no one will fall below the poverty line…this would be a great leap forward for humanity.

- Try to become self-sufficient as much as possible
- have your own vegetable urban garden
- cycle to work if possible

- buy what you need…eat healthy…drink in moderation
- save money…have a partner who is not a drain on your resources…if your partner has an income…combine the two incomes and have an investment plan
- the earlier you save the better your economic prospects
- no one can predict the future…be prepared…money in the bank will give you some financial security
- for women the best way to get rich…is marry a rich man...the standard way for women to get rich…and if you divorce him… you can be more rich…as you take 50% of everything he owns

In my next book on how business works I will tell the reality of starting...owning and running your own business...and it's not a get rich quick scheme.

Sources

Goodbye America…end of the $dollar Empire…M.Rowbotham

Dk.Publishing…how money works

The future of money…..M.Mellor

Cash less by R.Turrin

Money matters…D.Boyle

Money..JK.Galbraith

www.ingramcontent.com/pod-product-compliance
Lightning Source LLC
Chambersburg PA
CBHW071924210526
45479CB00002B/545